hamlyn

QuickCoo

Food for Friends

Recipes by Emma Lewis

Every dish, three ways – you choose!
30 minutes | 20 minutes | 10 minutes

An Hachette UK Company
www.hachette.co.uk

First published in Great Britain in 2013 by Hamlyn,
a division of Octopus Publishing Group Ltd
Endeavour House, 189 Shaftesbury Avenue
London WC2H 8JY
www.octopusbooks.co.uk

Copyright © Octopus Publishing Group Ltd 2013

ISBN 978-0-600-62582-7

A CIP catalogue record for this book is available from the British Library

Printed and bound in China

10 9 8 7 6 5 4 3 2 1

Both metric and imperial measurements are given for the recipes. Use one set of
measurements only, not a mixture of both.

Standard level spoon measurements are used in all recipes
1 tablespoon = 15 ml
1 teaspoon = 5 ml

Ovens should be preheated to the specified temperature. If using a fan-assisted oven,
follow the manufacturer's instructions for adjusting the time and temperature. Grills
should also be preheated.

This book includes dishes made with nuts and nut derivatives. It is advisable for
those with known allergic reactions to nuts and nut derivatives and those who may
be potentially vulnerable to these allergies, such as pregnant and nursing mothers,
invalids, the elderly, babies and children, to avoid dishes made with nuts and nut oils.

It is also prudent to check the labels of preprepared ingredients for the possible
inclusion of nut derivatives.

The Department of Health advises that eggs should not be consumed raw. This book
contains some dishes made with raw or lightly cooked eggs. It is prudent for more
vulnerable people such as pregnant and nursing mothers, invalids, the elderly, babies
and young children, as above to avoid uncooked or lightly cooked dishes made
with eggs.

Contents

Introduction

30 20 10 – Quick, Quicker, Quickest

This book offers a new and flexible approach to meal-planning for busy cooks and lets you choose the recipe option that best fits the time you have available. Inside you will find 360 dishes that will inspire you and motivate you to get cooking every day of the year. All the recipes take a maximum of 30 minutes to cook. Some take as little as 20 minutes and, amazingly, many take only 10 minutes. With a bit of preparation, you can easily try out one new recipe from this book each night and slowly you will build a wide and exciting portfolio of recipes to suit your needs.

How Does it Work?

Every recipe in the QuickCook series can be cooked one of three ways – a 30-minute version, a 20-minute version or a super-quick and easy 10-minute version. At the beginning of each chapter you'll find recipes listed by time. Choose a dish based on how much time you have and turn to that page.

You'll find the main recipe in the middle of the page with a beautiful photograph and two time-variations below.

If you enjoy the dish, you can go back and cook the other time options. If you liked the 20-minute Cod Fillets with Tomatoes and Salsa Verde (see pages 160–161), but only have 10 minutes to spare, then you'll find a way to cook it using cheat ingredients or clever shortcuts.

If you love the ingredients and flavours of the 10-minute Iced Berries with White Chocolate Sauce (see pages 240–241), why not try the 20-minute White Chocolate Berry Mousses, or be inspired to cook a more elaborate sweet treat using similar ingredients, such as the 30-minute White Chocolate and Berry Cookies. Alternatively, browse through all the 360 recipes, find something that catches your eye and then cook the version that fits your time frame.

Or, for easy inspiration, turn to the gallery on pages 12–19 to get an instant overview by themes, such as Special Occasions and Party Treats.

QuickCook Online

To make life even easier, you can use the special code on each recipe page to email yourself a recipe card for printing, or email a text-only shopping list to your phone. Go to www.hamlynquickcook.com and enter the recipe code at the bottom of each page.

  FOO-PUDD-FUA

QuickCook Food for Friends

Inviting friends and family over for a bite to eat should be the easiest, most enjoyable thing in the world, but too often most of your time is spent slaving in the kitchen rather than having fun and enjoying dinner together. But it's easy to produce delicious, inspiring dishes in less than 30 minutes, and some are so simple they can be on the table in just 10 minutes. Which lets you get on with the important things in life.

Get Ahead

A bit of planning ahead is always useful when having friends over. Once you've decided on a guest list, you need to organize a menu. Try to think of your guests' tastes – find out if you need to cater for any special diets or if there is something people especially love to eat – and then decide on your main course. Once you've worked this out, it's easier to decide what else to serve. Don't vary cooking styles too much: if you've decided on an Asian-influenced main course, try and work some of these flavours into the starter and pudding, too.

Think about timings when planning what you eat. For a larger meal, it's useful to actually write down a time plan of when things need to be started. But no matter the scale of your event, it's always best to cook a few delicious dishes rather than stress out trying to organize a large array of mediocre ones. It's a good idea to focus your effort on one dish, so if you choose a complicated starter, keep the main course simple, with something like pasta. If you choose a show-off pudding and main course, make the starter a no-cook salad.

When planning your menu, make sure you think about the washing up. You don't want to be cleaning up the kitchen for hours after your guests have left, so wash up as you go along. If time is really short, cook a one-pot dish: a smart pan that can be taken straight from the hob to the table is a great investment and makes for a relaxing meal.

Set the Scene

To welcome your guests, make sure your home looks its best. A quick tidy-up before everyone arrives is essential. Decide where you want to eat – maybe the kitchen for a casual dinner, the dining room for a more formal occasion or perhaps a buffet table if you have a lot of people coming. A vase of flowers is a quick and easy way of making any room look special. Buy cheap seasonal flowers to keep down costs, and if you're planning to put them on the table make sure they are low enough not to block guests' views of each other.

A beautiful tablecloth will make any meal feel more festive – an antique linen sheet makes a good-value tablecloth. Set the table with plain white china, or mix and match second-hand plates for a cheap and easy vintage look. If you're feeling creative, leaves, shells and ribbons can look very effective scattered on the table or arranged around the place settings, while fruits and vegetables can make a decorative centrepiece. Keep the lights in the room low for an inviting, intimate feel – you can place tea lights around the room or on the table, for example – but make sure it's not so dark that people can't see what they are eating. Finally, decide on what kind music you want to play to set the mood or get the party going. Just make sure the music is low enough for people to carry on conversations.

Stress-free Cooking
Starters
A sit-down starter sets the scene for a formal evening – perhaps a birthday dinner or when you want to impress the parents-in-law – and this book includes a tempting range of simple starter recipes. On other occasions, it is perfectly acceptable to abandon formal starters and set out a selection of nuts, olives and good-quality crisps, served with a cocktail or glass of bubbly. You could provide more substantial nibbles, to which guests can help themselves, such as hams and salami, sun-blush tomatoes, Crispy Tostados (see page 52), Red Pepper Dip (see page 64), Fig and Cheese Crostini (see page 40) or Roasted Aubergine Bruschetta (see page 30).

Main courses
There are plenty of ways of keeping the main course simple and quick. A leg or shoulder of lamb will take quite a while to cook in the oven, but a rack of lamb can be on the table in less

than 30 minutes. This makes life easy, but remember that with these leaner, quick-cooking cuts of meat, it really is worthwhile spending a bit extra to get the best quality – you will taste the difference. Fish and seafood are perfect for the host in a hurry as they take so little time to cook and need little more than a squeeze of lemon juice and simple side dish to turn them into a delicious dinner-party treat. Just remember to shop for them on the day you are planning to cook them, as fresh fish really does taste better.

Vegetarians can sometimes feel a bit cheated at dinner parties, so to make a meal really special, look out for seasonal ingredients – the first asparagus of the season or a perfectly ripe bunch of tomatoes make a great starting point for a meat-free meal. More unusual heritage vegetables or baby vegetables, which are now widely available, are also a wonderful way of perking up a plate and making it look worthy of a restaurant.

The flavour of good-quality basic ingredients will always shine through, and all it takes to enhance them is a little fresh pesto, a drizzle of special oil or vinegar or a scattering of herbs. Keep side dishes simple and fast – a selection of leaves dressed with something special, or maybe some couscous or polenta, which can be ready in 5 minutes flat. Make the most of tinned beans, which can be easily whizzed up to make a quick mash or you can toss them with some dressing and tomatoes to make a hearty salad.

Another way to make the meal a little more special is to use an unusual ingredient. Supermarkets are increasingly catering for our more exotic tastes and an exciting ingredient can make a meal really memorable. Look out for jewel-like pomegranate seeds, which look so pretty on the plate and are great to scatter over salads or Middle Eastern dishes. For an Asian dish, try to get some authentic ingredients like lime leaves and lemongrass, which will lend your dish a beautifully subtle and different flavour, or go to the trouble of tracking down an authentic curry paste. If you're making a simple Italian supper, search out a different type of pasta than you usually use – perhaps try thick tube-like bucatini or use black squid-ink pasta for a seafood dish. Sometimes, it is worth spending a little extra on a key ingredient that can be used sparingly. Creamy rich buffalo mozzarella is a world apart from the regular cow's milk version, while just a hint of perfumed saffron will transform a paella. It's also worth remembering that a splash of alcohol really helps to lift a dish – brandy or wine for a classic French dish, a drop of vermouth for fish or try something more unusual like sherry for a Spanish feel.

Pudding
To round off the meal in style you'll want to prepare something memorable, but this doesn't have to be complicated. Browse through the pudding recipes for inspiration, choosing a 10-minute recipe if you are short on time. Many of the quicker recipes are elegant enough to serve at a formal dinner, including Chocolate Soufflé Wraps (see page 234), Iced Berries with White Chocolate Sauce (see page 240), Lemon Baskets (see page 256) and Warm Mango and Raspberry Gratin (see page 274). For a really stress-free evening, serve a selection of great cheeses with some walnuts and perhaps a bottle of sweet wine, or a colourful bowl of exotic fruit salad.

What To Do If It All Goes Wrong
Even the best, most experienced cook will have nights when things go wrong in the kitchen. The most important thing is not to panic: a relaxed, welcoming host is what makes the evening. And the chances are that no one will notice anyway – a name change is often all that is needed. Your defrosted ice cream becomes a mousse, overcooked potatoes turn into instant mash and burnt onions are passed off as a caramelized onion sauce.

If in doubt, keep some cooked prawns and a tub of good vanilla ice cream on hand in the freezer and a bottle of bubbly in the fridge. Popping open the bubbly will keep your guests happy while you whip up a super-quick and delicious emergency dinner of prawns with pasta or a risotto followed by ice cream in next to no time.

Italian Favourites

Everyone loves Italian food, making it a great dinner-party choice

Clam Pasta with Tomatoes 54

Chicken Saltimbocca 86

Porcini Meatballs 118

Italian Fish Stew 142

Charred Tuna with Peperonata 154

Prosciutto-Wrapped Scallops with Peppers 168

Butternut Risotto with Chilli and Ricotta 190

Puttanesca Pizza 210

Aubergine, Tomato and Mozzarella Melts 222

Vanilla Baked Apricots with Ricotta Cream 236

Coffee Cocktail with Almond Biscuits 238

Raspberry Tiramisu 260

Spicy Favourites

Recipes to help you make the most of your spice rack

Chicken and Chermoula
Pilaff 82

Spicy Stir-Fried Chilli
Chicken 84

Pork and Pineapple Curry 100

Rack of Lamb with Harissa
Dressing 106

Beef Strips with Tomatoes,
Paprika and Onion 122

Seared Monkfish with Spiced
Beans 136

Tomato and Feta Pilaff with
Prawns 138

Tandoori Salmon with Yogurt
Sauce 140

Goan Prawn and Coconut
Curry 152

Spicy Tofu and Mushroom
Stir-Fry 186

Spicy Grilled Courgettes with
Hummus Mash 218

Cinnamon Plum Crumble 244

Light & Healthy

These fresh, tasty dishes are perfect for a light lunch

Celeriac Remoulade with Ham 38

Asparagus Mimosa 44

Crab and Mango Salad with Chilli Lime Dressing 48

Caesar Salad 60

Smoked Duck, Orange and Watercress Salad 88

Grilled Lamb with Minted Peas 104

Grilled Swordfish with Warm Romesco Salad 132

Thai-Style Squid Salad 156

Tea-Smoked Salmon 166

Sesame-Crusted Tuna with Ginger Dressing 170

Sweet Potato Laksa 196

Miso Aubergine with Cucumber Rice Noodles 202

Hearty & Substantial

Wholesome food to make your guests feel welcome

Chicken, Leek and Tarragon Pie 78

Herbed Pork with Creamy Apple Sauce 98

Seared Beef Fillet with Horseradish Sauce 120

Manhattan Clam Chowder 134

Two-Bean Chilli with Avocado Salsa 194

Pepper and Artichoke Paella 198

Puffed Goats' Cheese and Red Pepper Omelettes 206

Carrot and Beetroot Tabbouleh 212

Mushroom Risotto with Gremolata 220

Molten Chocolate Cakes 234

Warm Almond Cakes with Fig Compote 242

Sticky Orange and Cinnamon Puddings 276

Special Occasions

Rise to the occasion with the very best ingredients

Crispy Bacon Oysters 42

Whole Baked Brie with Pecans and Maple Syrup 50

Salmon Carpaccio with Beetroot Topping 56

Saffron Roasted Chicken 80

Lamb and Pepper Tray Bake with Mint Salsa 110

Individual Beef Wellingtons 112

Sea Bream in a Salt Fennel Crust with Lemon Dressing 130

Grilled Lobster with Herb Butter 174

Baked Tomato and Spinach Puffs 180

Strawberry Meringue Roulade 232

Banana Pecan Strudels 254

Warm Chocolate Cherry Tarts 270

Party Treats

Bite-sized snacks and food designed for sharing

Bloody Mary Gazpacho 26

Baked Mushrooms with Taleggio and Pesto 34

Three Cheese Filo Bites 40

Chicken Liver Pâté 68

Vietnamese Beef Skewers 114

Crab and Corn Cakes with Red Pepper Mayonnaise 144

Smoked Haddock and Spinach Tart 150

Citrus-Roasted Salmon 172

Leek and Blue Cheese Tart 204

Chocolate Peanut Butter Whoopie Pies 250

Strawberry Rhubarb Shortcake Slices 266

Honey Ricotta Fritters with Pistachios 278

Relaxed and Informal

Easy-going dishes for a kitchen-table supper

Spanish Prawns with Chorizo 36

Turkish Pizza with Spinach, Pomegranate and Feta 46

Crispy Tostados with Avocado and Tomatoes 52

Red Pepper Dip with Herb Pitta Crackers 64

Roasted Chicken Breasts with Herb Butter 76

Mustard Rarebit-Style Pork Chops 90

Lamb Steaks with Tomatoes, Feta and Hummus Mash 108

Grilled Rib-Eye Steak 116

Chickpea Falafel Wraps 188

Sticky Toffee Cakes 246

Individual Pear Crumbles with Flapjack Topping 252

Caramelized Custard Tarts 268

Someone to Impress

Delicious show-stoppers worthy of your best china

Squid with Lemon and Capers 32

Blue Cheese Soufflé with Apple and Rocket 58

Thai Pork with Mango Salsa 94

Seared Prawns with Squid Ink Pasta 128

Hot-Smoked Salmon and Watercress Pasta 146

Roasted Hake with Tomatoes and Pistou 148

Salmon, Dill and Rice Parcels 162

Baked Sea Bass with Tomatoes, Olives and Oregano 164

Chargrilled Haloumi with Roasted Olives and Salad 208

Lemon Puddings 256

White Chocolate Rice Pudding Brûlée 262

Passionfruit Cheesecakes 272

QuickCook
Starters

Recipes listed by cooking time

30

20

Baked Figs Wrapped in Prosciutto

Serves 4

8 figs
125 g (4 oz) mozzarella cheese,
   cut into 8 slices
8 slices of prosciutto
7 tablespoons olive oil
2 tablespoons balsamic vinegar
125 g (4 oz) rocket leaves
salt and pepper

· Cut a deep cross into the top of each fig, nearly to the bottom, then place a piece of mozzarella inside. Wrap a slice of prosciutto around each fig. Brush the prosciutto with a little oil. Transfer to a baking sheet and cook in a preheated oven, 220°C (425°F), Gas Mark 7, for 7–10 minutes or until the ham is crisp and the cheese starts to melt.

· Meanwhile, whisk together the balsamic vinegar with the remaining oil and season well. Toss most of the dressing together with the rocket leaves and arrange on plates. Add the figs and drizzle with a little more of the dressing. Serve immediately.

Fig and Ham Country Salad

Halve 8 figs and brush them with a little olive oil. Heat a griddle pan until smoking and then cook the cut sides of the figs for 1 minute until lightly charred. Wrap each half in a slice of prosciutto. Mix 1 tablespoon finely chopped shallot with 1 tablespoon sherry vinegar and 3 tablespoons olive oil. Toss through 150 g (5 oz) salad leaves and serve with the griddled figs with some soft goats' cheese crumbled on top.

Fig Tatin with Ham

From a 375 g (12 oz) sheet of ready-rolled pastry, cut out 4 circles, about 10 cm (4 inches) across. Heat 4 tablespoons sugar with 2 teaspoons water in a small pan. Allow the mixture to bubble and turn a dark caramel colour. Remove the saucepan from the heat and stir in 2 tablespoons red wine vinegar. Pour the mixture into the bottoms of 4 individual Yorkshire pudding tins. Slice 8 figs and place them on top. Put the pastry circles on top of the figs and bake in a preheated oven, 200°C (400°F), Gas Mark 6, for 15–20 minutes until the pastry is golden. Invert the tarts on to plates and top each with some rocket leaves, a slice of Parma ham and some shaved Manchego cheese.

10 Bloody Mary Gazpacho

Serves 4

2 garlic cloves, chopped

2 celery sticks, chopped, plus extra to serve

1 tablespoon chopped onion

500 g (1 lb) ripe tomatoes

300 ml (½ pint) tomato juice

juice of 2 limes

1 teaspoon celery salt

2–3 tablespoons Worcestershire sauce

125 ml (4 fl oz) vodka (optional)

Tabasco sauce, to taste

lime wedges, to serve

- Put all the ingredients, except the vodka and Tabasco sauce, in a food processor and whizz until smooth. Press the mixture through a fine sieve.

- Add the vodka, if using, and Tabasco sauce to taste and pour into glasses. Serve with sprigs of celery and lime wedges.

---

20 Pitta Crisps with Gazpacho Salsa

Cut 4 pitta breads into thick strips. Toss them together with 2 tablespoons olive oil, spread them out on a baking sheet and cook in a preheated oven, 190°C (375°F), Gas Mark 5, for 7–10 minutes until golden and crisp. Leave to cool. Meanwhile, finely chop 4 tomatoes, ¼ cucumber and ½ red pepper and toss together with 2 crushed garlic cloves, 1 tablespoon sherry vinegar and 3 tablespoons extra virgin olive oil. Serve the salsa with the pitta crisps.

30 Roasted Tomato Gazpacho

Toss 500 g (1 lb) halved tomatoes with 3 tablespoons olive oil. Place in a roasting tin with 2 garlic cloves and cook in a preheated oven, 200°C (400°F), Gas Mark 6, for 20 minutes or until soft and lightly browned. Place in a blender with 1 ready-roasted red pepper, 2 teaspoons sherry vinegar, 1 crustless slice of bread and 300 ml (½ pint) tomato juice and whizz until smooth. Rub through a sieve to remove all the pulp, then season and add a little Tabasco sauce to taste. Chill in the freezer for 5 minutes, then ladle into serving bowls. Scatter over 1 tablespoon chopped red onion mixed together with 1 diced avocado.

Spiced Coconut Squash Soup

Serves 4–6

2 tablespoons oil

1 onion, chopped

2 teaspoons finely chopped fresh
   root ginger

½ teaspoon ground coriander

1 lemon grass stalk

1 strip of orange peel

1 kg (2 lb) butternut squash,
   peeled and chopped

1 litre (1¾ pints) vegetable stock

125 ml (4 fl oz) coconut milk

salt and pepper

To serve

1 red chilli, chopped

fresh coriander leaves, chopped

- Heat the oil in a large saucepan, add the onion and cook for 5 minutes until softened. Add the ginger, ground coriander, lemon grass, orange peel and squash. Pour in the stock and coconut milk and bring to the boil. Leave to simmer for 12–15 minutes until the squash is soft.

- Remove the lemon grass and orange peel and use a stick blender to whizz to a smooth paste. Season to taste and divide between serving bowls. Sprinkle over the chilli and fresh coriander to serve.

Griddled Squash and Coconut Salad

Peel and thinly slice ½ butternut squash. Toss with 2 tablespoons oil, then season and cook on a griddle pan for 2–3 minutes on each side until charred and soft. Whisk together 3 tablespoons lime juice with 4 tablespoons oil and 1 finely chopped chilli. Toss the squash together with 150 g (5 oz) salad leaves, a handful of fresh coriander and the dressing. Scatter with toasted desiccated coconut to serve.

Coconut Squash Rice Pot

Heat 2 tablespoons oil in a large saucepan, add 1 chopped onion and cook for 5 minutes until softened. Stir in 1 crushed garlic clove and 1 teaspoon finely chopped fresh root ginger, followed by 2 tablespoons Thai red curry paste. Add ½ peeled and chopped butternut squash and cook for a couple of minutes until well coated. Stir through 300 g (10 oz) jasmine rice. Pour over 500 ml (17 fl oz) vegetable stock and 125 ml (4 fl oz) coconut milk. Bring to the boil and cook for 10 minutes, then reduce the heat and simmer gently for 5 minutes until the rice and squash are just cooked through. Scatter over a handful chopped fresh coriander leaves before serving.

FOO-STAR-VUA

30 Charred Aubergine and Tomato Quesadillas

Serves 4

1 aubergine, sliced
4 tablespoons olive oil
1 onion, sliced
1 garlic clove, crushed
pinch of cayenne powder
1 tablespoon tomato purée
6 tomatoes, chopped
4 soft flour tortillas
75 g (3 oz) soft goats' cheese
salt and pepper

- Toss the aubergine together with 2 tablespoons oil and season with salt and pepper. Heat a griddle pan until smoking hot, then cook the aubergine for 3 minutes on each side until charred and soft.

- Heat the remaining oil in a saucepan, add the onion and cook over a low heat for 10 minutes until soft. Stir in the garlic, followed by the cayenne, tomato purée and tomatoes. Leave to cook for 5–10 minutes until the tomatoes are lightly charred.

- Lay the tortillas on a work surface. Spoon some tomatoes over one half of each tortilla, add some aubergine slices and crumble over some goats' cheese. Fold each tortilla in half, transfer to a baking sheet and place under a hot grill for 2–3 minutes. Carefully turn over and cook for 2–3 minutes more until golden and crispy all over. Cut into wedges and serve.

---

10 Roasted Aubergine Bruschetta

Thickly slice 1 ciabatta loaf, rub the cut sides with 2 tablespoons olive oil, then cook under a medium-hot grill for 2–3 minutes on each side until golden and crisp. Rub the surface of each toast with a peeled garlic clove. Toss 75 g (3 oz) chopped ready-roasted aubergine with 4 chopped tomatoes, 1 teaspoon balsamic vinegar, 2 tablespoons olive oil and a handful of chopped basil. Spoon over the ciabatta and top with a little soft goats' cheese before serving.

20 Charred Aubergine, Tomato and Goats' Cheese Pasta

Thickly slice 1 aubergine, toss together with 4 tablespoons olive oil and place on a baking sheet. Cook in a preheated oven, 220°C (425°F), Gas Mark 7, for 10 minutes. Add 125 g (4 oz) halved cherry tomatoes and cook for 5 minutes more until lightly charred and soft. Heat a large pan of salted water and cook 300 g (10 oz) penne pasta according to the pack instructions. Drain and return the pasta to the pan. Stir in 2 teaspoons balsamic vinegar, the aubergine and tomatoes and any juices. Divide between 4 serving bowls and scatter over 50 g (2 oz) grated hard goats' cheese and a handful of chopped basil.

 # Squid with Lemon and Capers

Serves 4–6

400 g (13 oz) prepared squid
4 tablespoons plain flour
4 tablespoons cornflour
1 tablespoon capers, drained and
　roughly chopped, plus extra
　whole capers to serve
finely grated rind and juice of
　1 large lemon
6 tablespoons mayonnaise
2 garlic cloves, crushed
oil, for frying
salt and pepper

· Cut the squid pouches in half. Score a criss-cross pattern across the inside of the squid with a sharp knife, taking care not to cut all the way through, then cut into bite-sized pieces. Mix together the plain flour, cornflour, chopped capers and lemon rind on a plate and season well.

· Toss the squid in the flour mixture, making sure it is well coated. Heat a large saucepan one-third full of oil. Test to see if it is hot enough by dropping a small piece of bread into it: it should sizzle and brown after 15 seconds. Cook the squid, in batches, for 2 minutes until golden and crisp, then set aside on kitchen paper. Briefly fry the whole capers and set aside on kitchen paper.

· Stir together the mayonnaise and garlic and add lemon juice to taste. Scatter some fried capers over the squid and serve with the mayonnaise for dipping.

 Grilled Squid and Citrus Salad

Halve 200 g (7 oz) baby squid, score the inside as above and cut into bite-sized pieces. Toss the squid with 1 tablespoon olive oil and season well. Cook on a smoking hot griddle pan for 1–2 minutes until lightly charred. Mix 2 tablespoons lemon juice, a pinch of ground sumac and 3 tablespoons olive oil and season to taste. Cut 1 orange into segments and toss with 150 g (5 oz) rocket. Stir the dressing through the salad and arrange on a plate with the squid. Scatter over 1 finely chopped red chilli to serve.

 Squid Ink Risotto with Lemon

Heat 2 tablespoons olive oil in a saucepan, add 1 finely chopped onion and cook for 5 minutes until softened. Add 2 finely chopped garlic cloves and cook for 30 seconds. Add 250 g (8 oz) risotto rice and stir around the pan. Pour 125 ml (4 fl oz) dry white wine into the pan and cook until it has bubbled away. Bring 400 ml (14 fl oz) fish or vegetable stock to the boil in a pan, then add 1 tablespoon squid ink. Gradually stir in the hot stock, a little at a time, stirring frequently and allowing the rice to absorb the stock before

adding more. Meanwhile, heat 1 tablespoon olive oil in a frying pan. Cut 150 g (5 oz) squid into rings, season and add to the frying pan. Cook for 2 minutes until lightly browned, then remove from the pan. When the rice is soft, after about 15 minutes, add the juice of 1 lemon and the cooked squid and serve scattered with a handful of chopped parsley.

Baked Mushrooms with Taleggio and Pesto

Serves 4

8 large flat mushrooms, stalks
  trimmed
8 slices of Taleggio cheese
75 g (3 oz) dried breadcrumbs
1 garlic clove, crushed
6 tablespoons olive oil
bunch of basil leaves, finely
  chopped
25 g (1 oz) Parmesan cheese,
  finely grated
25 g (1 oz) toasted pine nuts,
  chopped, plus extra to serve
salt and pepper

- Put the mushrooms on a baking sheet and top each one with a slice of Taleggio. Mix together the breadcrumbs and garlic and scatter a little over each mushroom. Drizzle with olive oil and bake in a preheated oven, 200°C (400°F), Gas Mark 6, for 15–20 minutes until golden and crispy.

- Meanwhile, mix together the basil, Parmesan, pine nuts and remaining oil and season to taste. Drizzle the pesto over the mushrooms and scatter over a few extra pine nuts to serve.

Grilled Mushroom Melts

Heat 1 tablespoon oil in a nonstick frying pan, add 150 g (5 oz) sliced mushrooms and cook for 3–5 minutes until softened. Add 1 crushed garlic clove. Meanwhile, lightly toast 2 halved individual baguettes and arrange, cut side up, on a baking sheet. Spoon over the mushrooms and top with 125 g (4 oz) grated Cheddar cheese. Cook under a hot grill for 2–3 minutes until the cheese has melted, then drizzle with 4 tablespoons fresh pesto to serve.

Leek and Mushroom Bake

Heat 2 tablespoons oil in a frying pan, add 1 thinly sliced leek and 125 g (4 oz) sliced mushrooms and cook for 3–5 minutes until softened. Whisk 6 eggs with 50 ml (2 fl oz) double cream and a handful of chopped basil and stir in the vegetables. Season to taste and pour the mixture into a greased 20 cm (8 inch) square cake tin. Scatter over 25 g (1 oz) grated Parmesan cheese and bake in a preheated oven, 180°C (350°F), Gas Mark 4, for 25 minutes until just set.

1 Spanish Prawns with Chorizo

Serves 4

1 tablespoon olive oil
150 g (5 oz) chorizo, thickly sliced
2 garlic cloves, sliced
250 g (8 oz) large raw peeled
 prawns
50 ml (2 fl oz) dry sherry
handful of chopped parsley
salt and pepper
crusty bread, to serve

- Heat the olive oil in a large frying pan, add the chorizo and cook for 1 minute on each side until just golden and crisp. Remove from the pan. Add the garlic and cook for 30 seconds. Then add the prawns and cook for 3 minutes until golden.

- Return the chorizo to the pan and carefully pour over the sherry. Season to taste with salt and pepper. Cook for 1 minute, then scatter over the parsley and serve with plenty of crusty bread.

2 Couscous Salad with Chorizo

and Prawns In a large pan heat 1 tablespoon olive oil, add 1 finely chopped onion and cook for 5 minutes until softened. Stir in 1 finely chopped garlic clove and cook for 30 seconds. Stir in 200 g (7 oz) couscous and a 200 g (7 oz) can rinsed and drained chickpeas, followed by 300 ml (½ pint) hot chicken stock. Remove the pan from the heat, cover and leave to cool. Add 2 tablespoons lemon juice and 2 more tablespoons olive oil, then stir in 125 g (4 oz) cooked peeled prawns and 75 g (3 oz) cooked chopped chorizo. Season and add a large handful of chopped parsley before serving.

3 Garlicky Prawn and Chorizo Pizza

Mix a 150 g (5 oz) pack of pizza base mix according to the pack instructions and knead for 3 minutes. Roll out into a round and leave to rise on a baking sheet lightly dusted with flour for 5 minutes. Spoon over 125 g (4 oz) fresh tomato pasta sauce. Arrange 150 g (5 oz) large cooked peeled prawns on top together with 6 slices of chorizo. Mix together 1 crushed garlic clove with 1 tablespoon olive oil and drizzle over the top. Bake in a preheated oven, 220°C (425°F), Gas Mark 7, for 15 minutes or until crisp. Scatter over a handful of rocket leaves and serve.

Celeriac Remoulade with Ham

Serves 6

5 tablespoons mayonnaise
1 tablespoon Dijon mustard
2 tablespoons crème fraîche
1 small celeriac, peeled and cut into fine matchsticks
handful of parsley, finely chopped
6 slices of Bayonne or Parma ham
salt and pepper

- Mix together the mayonnaise, mustard and crème fraîche until smooth. Season to taste, then stir together with the celeriac and parsley.
- Spoon the mixture on to serving plates along with the ham.

 Celeriac Remoulade and Ham Rolls Whisk together 2 egg yolks with 1 teaspoon Dijon mustard, then slowly whisk in 300 ml (½ pint) olive oil, at first one drop at a time, until creamy. Season to taste with lemon juice and salt and pepper. Stir through 1 tablespoon drained capers and a handful each of chopped parsley and chives. Cut ½ celeriac into thin matchsticks and stir together with the mayonnaise. Spoon a little of the celeriac on to one end of a slice of ham and roll up, repeating to make 12 rolls. Arrange them on a plate with sprigs of watercress.

 Celeriac Soup with Crispy Ham Heat 1 tablespoon oil in a large saucepan, add 1 finely chopped onion and cook for 5 minutes until softened. Add 1 chopped celeriac and 1 chopped potato. Pour over 1.5 litres (2½ pints) chicken stock and add the finely grated rind of ½ lemon. Bring to the boil, then reduce the heat and simmer for 20 minutes until soft. Use a stick blender to whizz to a smooth soup and season to taste. Meanwhile, heat 1 tablespoon oil in a small frying pan, add 4 slices of Parma ham and cook for 1–2 minutes until just crispy. Add 2–3 sage leaves and fry for 30 seconds until crisp. Ladle the soup into bowls and top with some crumbled ham and sage leaves and a sprinkling of finely grated Parmesan cheese.

FOO-STAR-VOG

30 Three Cheese Filo Bites

Serves 6

125 g (4 oz) feta cheese
125 g (4 oz) ricotta cheese
50 g (2 oz) grated Pecorino cheese
2 eggs, beaten
100 g (3½ oz) butter, melted
4 tablespoons olive oil, plus extra for greasing
4 large sheets of filo pastry
salt and pepper

- Drain any excess water from the feta and ricotta, then mix together with the Pecorino and eggs. Season to taste. Stir together the butter and olive oil. Unwrap the filo pastry, keeping any pastry you are not using covered with a damp (but not wet) tea towel.

- Cut each pastry sheet into thirds lengthways and brush all over with the butter mixture. Place a heaped spoonful of the cheese mixture at one end of a strip of pastry. Fold one corner of the pastry diagonally over the filling to meet the other side, then continue to fold all the way down the strip to create a triangular parcel. Repeat with the remaining pastry and ingredients.

- Place the parcels on a lightly greased baking sheet, brush over again with the butter and oil and bake in a preheated oven, 200°C (400°F), Gas Mark 6, for 12 minutes or until golden and crisp. Serve warm from the oven.

1 Fig and Cheese Crostini

Cut ½ baguette into slices and lightly toast. Mix together 100 g (3½ oz) ricotta with 75 g (3 oz) feta cheese and spoon over the toasts. Slice 4 figs and arrange on top of the cheese. Use a vegetable peeler to shave a little Pecorino over each crostini to serve.

2 Tomato and Three Cheese Fritters

Mix together 250 g (8 oz) drained ricotta with 1 beaten egg, 75 g (3 oz) chopped sun-dried tomatoes, 1 crushed garlic clove and 25 g (1 oz) finely grated Pecorino. Stir through 50 g (2 oz) plain flour. Heat a large, nonstick frying pan, add a little olive oil and then drop spoonfuls of the cheese mixture into the pan. Cook for 2 minutes on each side until golden and cooked through. Arrange on plates with a handful of rocket leaves and sliced cucumber. Drizzle over 1 tablespoon olive oil and 2 teaspoons balsamic vinegar, then scatter over 50 g (2 oz) feta and a handful of chopped fresh oregano.

2 Crispy Bacon Oysters

Serves 4

2 tablespoons olive oil
200 g (7 oz) baby spinach leaves
1 spring onion, sliced
1 garlic clove, crushed
2 tablespoons crème fraîche
4 rashers of bacon
12 oysters
50 g (2 oz) dried breadcrumbs
pinch of cayenne
salt and pepper

- Heat 1 tablespoon oil in a frying pan, add the spinach leaves and cook for 1 minute until starting to wilt. Add the spring onion and garlic and cook for 1 minute more until wilted. Pour away any excess water, then stir in the crème fraîche.

- Meanwhile, grill the bacon for 5–8 minutes until crisp, then cut into small pieces. Open the oysters, discarding the top shell, and arrange them on a baking sheet. Spoon over some of the spinach mixture (together with any oyster juices) and add some bacon pieces. Mix the breadcrumbs with the cayenne and sprinkle over the top.

- Drizzle over the remaining oil and bake in a preheated oven, 230°C (450°F), Gas Mark 8, for 10 minutes or until the breadcrumbs are crisp.

 Smoked Oyster and Spinach Omelette Heat a large frying pan, add 125 g (4 oz) baby spinach leaves and 1 sliced garlic clove and cook for 2 minutes until wilted. Remove from the pan and wipe it clean. Whisk together 4 eggs and 1 egg yolk. Add one-quarter of the egg to the pan and swirl around. When it is just starting to set, sprinkle over one-quarter of the cooked spinach, one-quarter of a can of smoked oysters, drained, and a few pieces of sliced Parma ham. Roll up and repeat to make 4 omelettes.

 Spinach and Oyster Bisque Heat 1 tablespoon oil in a large pan, add 2 sliced bacon rashers and cook for 5 minutes until browned. Remove from the pan. Add 1 finely chopped onion and 1 finely chopped leek and cook over a low heat for 5 minutes until softened. Remove from the pan. Melt 2 tablespoons butter in the pan, then stir in 1 tablespoon plain flour and cook for 2 minutes, stirring often. Pour in 150 ml (5 fl oz) vegetable stock, whisking together until smooth. Then whisk in 1.5 litres (2½ pints) more stock and a splash of Pernod, if liked. Return the vegetables to the pan and bring to the boil. Reduce the heat and simmer for 10 minutes. Shuck 12 oysters. Add 8 along with the juices to the soup together with 300 g (10 oz) baby spinach leaves. Cook for 1 minute, then whizz in a food processor until smooth. Return to the pan and stir in 100 ml (3½ fl oz) double cream and the bacon and heat through. Put the remaining oysters into serving bowls, ladle over the soup and serve straight away.

FOO-STAR-CUO

 Asparagus Mimosa

Serves 4

6 quails' or 2 hens' eggs
200 g (7 oz) asparagus
1 teaspoon Dijon mustard
1 tablespoon white wine vinegar
1 tablespoon single cream
75 ml (3 fl oz) olive oil
1 tablespoon capers, drained
50 g (2 oz) pitted black olives, chopped
salt and pepper

- Bring a pan of water to the boil and gently lower in the eggs. Cook the quails' eggs for 5 minutes and the hens' eggs for 8 minutes. Remove from the pan and cool under cold running water. Cook the asparagus in a pan of lightly salted boiling water for 3–5 minutes until just tender, drain and cool under cold running water.

- Stir together the mustard, vinegar and cream and then slowly whisk in the oil, a little at a time. Season well.

- Arrange the asparagus on 4 plates and drizzle over the dressing. Roughly chop the eggs and scatter over the asparagus together with the capers and olives.

 Asparagus with Soft Boiled Egg

Cook 150 g (5 oz) asparagus tips in a pan of lightly salted boiling water for 2–3 minutes until just tender and then remove from the pan. Bring the water back to the boil and add 4 eggs. Leave to cook for 4 minutes until soft boiled. Place in egg cups and slice off the tops. Wrap a strip of smoked salmon around each asparagus tip and use them to dip into the eggs.

Asparagus Tart

Mix together 2 eggs with 150 g (5 oz) mascarpone cheese and 50 g (2 oz) grated Parmesan. Place a 375 g (12 oz) sheet of ready-rolled puff pastry on a lightly greased baking sheet. Score a 1 cm (½ inch) border around the pastry. Spread the egg mixture all over the pastry inside the border, then arrange 200 g (7 oz) asparagus spears on top together with 25 g (1 oz) roughly chopped black olives. Drizzle over 1 tablespoon olive oil and bake in a preheated oven, 200°C (400°F), Gas Mark 6, for 15–20 minutes until golden and puffed.

3 ⬤ Turkish Pizza with Spinach, Pomegranate and Feta

Serves 4

2 x 150 g (5 oz) packs pizza base mix
1 tablespoon olive oil, plus extra for greasing
2 garlic cloves, sliced
250 g (8 oz) baby spinach leaves
125 g (4 oz) feta cheese
50 g (2 oz) pomegranate seeds
salt and pepper

- Mix the pizza base according to the pack instructions and knead for 3 minutes. Divide the dough into 4 pieces, roll out each piece into an oval shape and place on a lightly greased baking sheet. Leave to rise for 5–10 minutes.

- Meanwhile, heat the oil in a frying pan, add the garlic and cook for a couple of seconds. Add the spinach and cook for 3 minutes until wilted. Season well and squeeze away any excess water.

- Arrange the spinach on the pizza bases, leaving a 1.5 cm (¾ inch) border. Fold in the long edges of the pizza and twist the ends. Sprinkle over the feta and bake in a preheated oven, 200°C (400°F), Gas Mark 6, for 15–20 minutes until the pizza is crisp and cooked through. Scatter over the pomegranate seeds before serving.

1 ◔ Spinach and Feta Salad with Pitta Chips

Split 2 pittas open horizontally and cut each half into wedges. Brush all over with 2 tablespoons olive oil and place in a preheated oven, 200°C (400°F), Gas Mark 6, for 5–7 minutes or until golden and crisp. Whisk together 1 crushed garlic clove with 1 tablespoon white wine vinegar and 3 tablespoons olive oil. Toss together with 150 g (5 oz) baby spinach leaves. Transfer to serving plates and arrange the pitta crisps, 50 g (2 oz) crumbled feta cheese and 25 g (1 oz) pomegranate seeds on top.

2 ◑ Spinach and Feta Dip with Grilled Flatbreads

Heat 1 tablespoon olive oil in a large saucepan, add 1 finely chopped onion and cook for 5 minutes until softened. Add 250 g (8 oz) baby spinach leaves to the saucepan with a splash of water. Cover and leave to cook, stirring occasionally, for 2 minutes until wilted. Squeeze away any water and leave to cool. Place in a food processor with 250 g (8 oz) ricotta, 200 g (7 oz) feta cheese, 1 crushed garlic clove and a squeeze of lemon juice and process until smooth. Brush 1 tablespoon olive oil over 4 lavash or large pitta breads. Heat a griddle pan until smoking hot and cook the breads for 1–2 minutes on each side until lightly charred. Serve with the dip.

10 Crab and Mango Salad with Chilli Lime Dressing

Serves 4

50 g (2 oz) caster sugar
75 ml (3 fl oz) water
2 tablespoons mirin
1 red chilli, sliced
1 kaffir lime leaf, shredded
finely grated rind and juice of
  1 lime
1 mango, peeled, pitted and
  chopped
75 g (3 oz) radishes, halved
¼ cucumber, sliced
125 g (4 oz) watercress
200 g (7 oz) freshly picked
  crab meat

- Put the sugar, water and mirin in a small saucepan, bring to the boil and cook for 3 minutes until it starts to turn syrupy. Stir in the chilli, lime leaf and lime rind and add lime juice to taste. Set aside for 5 minutes.

- Toss together the mango, radishes, cucumber and watercress and arrange on serving plates. Sprinkle the crab meat on top and then drizzle over the dressing.

2 Thai Crab Cakes with Mango Salsa

Mix together 400 g (13 oz) freshly picked crab meat with 2 teaspoons Thai red curry paste, 1 tablespoon Thai fish sauce and just enough beaten egg white to bring the mixture together. Lightly wet your hands and shape into small cakes. Heat 1 tablespoon oil in a nonstick frying pan, add the crab cakes and cook for 3 minutes on each side until golden and just cooked through. Meanwhile, peel and finely chop the flesh of ½ mango and mix with 1 tablespoon finely chopped red onion, ½ finely chopped red chilli, a good squeeze of lime juice and a handful of chopped fresh coriander. Spoon the salsa over the crab cakes to serve.

3 Wild Rice, Crab and Mango Salad

Bring a large pan of lightly salted water to the boil, add 200 g (7 oz) mixed wild and basmati rice and cook for 25 minutes or according to the pack instructions. Drain and rinse under cold running water to cool. Meanwhile, mix 1 tablespoon finely chopped red onion with 1 teaspoon finely chopped fresh root ginger, 1 finely chopped red chilli, the juice and finely grated rind of 1 lime and 3 tablespoons olive oil. Add the rice, a large handful of chopped fresh coriander, 1 peeled and chopped mango and 150 g (5 oz) picked fresh crab meat, stir well and serve.

Whole Baked Brie with Pecans and Maple Syrup

Serves 4

300 g (10 oz) whole baby Brie or Camembert
25 g (1 oz) pecans
3 tablespoons maple syrup
3 tablespoons soft brown sugar
thyme sprigs
crusty bread, to serve

- Remove any plastic packaging from the cheese and return it to its wooden box. Place on a baking sheet and cook in a preheated oven, 200°C (400°F), Gas Mark 6, for 15 minutes.

- Meanwhile, toast the pecans in a small frying pan for 3–5 minutes until lightly browned, then set aside. Put the maple syrup and sugar in a small saucepan and bring to the boil. Cook for 1 minute until foamy.

- Take the cheese from the oven and cut a small cross in the centre. Drizzle over the maple syrup, scatter with the pecans and thyme and serve with plenty of crusty bread.

 Brie Salad with Maple Dressing
Whisk together 1 tablespoon maple syrup with 1 teaspoon mustard, 1 tablespoon white wine vinegar and 3 tablespoons olive oil. Season and toss together with 200 g (7 oz) mixed salad leaves. Arrange on plates with 25 g (1 oz) toasted pecans. Cut 125 g (4 oz) Brie into thick slices. Put the Brie on a baking sheet and cook under a hot grill for 1 minute or until starting to melt. Scatter over the salad to serve.

Brie en Croûte with Cranberries, Maple Syrup and Pecans Slice a whole baby Brie, about 300 g (10 oz), in half horizontally. Scatter 25 g (1 oz) dried cranberries and a handful of chopped pecans over one half, then drizzle with 2 tablespoons maple syrup. Put the other half back on top. Cut out 2 rounds from a 375 g (12 oz) sheet of ready-rolled puff pastry, one slightly larger than the other, to accommodate the Brie. Put the Brie on the smaller round and brush the pastry edges with 1 beaten egg. Put the other pastry round on top and press the edges together with your fingers. Brush over more egg and cook in a preheated oven, 220°C (425°F), Gas Mark 7, for 10 minutes. Turn the oven down to 180°C (350°F), Gas Mark 4, and cook for 10–15 minutes more until puffed and golden.

10 Crispy Tostados with Avocado and Tomatoes

Serves 4

4 corn tortillas
1 tablespoon vegetable oil
2 avocadoes, peeled and pitted
50 ml (2 fl oz) crème fraîche
2–3 tablespoons lime juice
4 tomatoes, chopped
1 tablespoon finely chopped red
   onion
1 tablespoon extra virgin olive oil
handful of fresh coriander,
   chopped, plus extra to serve
   (optional)
salt and pepper

- Use a 5 cm (2 inch) biscuit cutter to stamp out rounds from the tortillas; alternatively, cut them into wedges. Brush them with vegetable oil, place on a baking sheet under a preheated hot grill and cook for 1 minute on each side until crisp. Leave to cool.

- Meanwhile, place the avocado flesh and crème fraîche in a food processor and blend until smooth. Stir in 1 tablespoon of lime juice and season to taste. Stir together the tomatoes, onion and olive oil, add lime juice to taste, season and stir through the coriander. Spoon a little of the avocado mixture on to each tortilla round, scatter over the tomato salsa and top with more coriander, if liked.

20 Crispy Baked Avocado with Tomatoes

Slice 2 avocados in half and remove the stones. Scoop out the flesh, setting aside the shells, and roughly mash. Grill 2 rashers of bacon for 5–7 minutes until just crisp, then chop into small pieces. Stir through the avocado with 1 chopped tomato and a handful of chopped coriander. Spoon the mixture into the shells and place on a baking sheet. Scatter over 50 g (2 oz) grated Cheddar cheese and 25 g (1 oz) crushed corn tortilla chips. Bake in a preheated oven, 200°C (400°F), Gas Mark 6, for 10 minutes or until the cheese has melted.

30 Tomato and Tortilla Soup

Heat 1 tablespoon olive oil in a saucepan, add 1 finely chopped onion and cook for 5 minutes until softened. Add 3 finely chopped garlic cloves and stir around the pan. Add 2 teaspoons chipotle purée, 400 g (13 oz) can chopped tomatoes, 1 teaspoon brown sugar and a pinch of dried oregano. Pour over 1 litre (1¾ pints) chicken or vegetable stock, bring to the boil, reduce the heat and simmer for 10 minutes. Use a stick blender to whizz together until smooth, then season to taste. Cut 2 corn tortillas into thin strips. Heat a large frying pan, add 1 tablespoon vegetable oil and cook the tortillas for 1–2 minutes until golden and crisp. Spoon the soup into bowls. Top with the chopped flesh of 1 avocado, 50 g (2 oz) crumbled feta, the crisp tortillas and a handful of chopped fresh coriander.

1 Clam Pasta with Tomatoes

Serves 4

3 tablespoons olive oil
2 garlic cloves, sliced
finely grated rind and juice of
  ½ lemon
3 canned anchovy fillets
125 ml (4 fl oz) dry white wine
pinch of dried chilli flakes
150 g (5 oz) cherry tomatoes,
  halved
500 g (1 lb) clams, scrubbed
500 g (1 lb) fresh spaghetti
75 g (3 oz) rocket
salt and pepper

· Heat the olive oil in a large saucepan, add the garlic, lemon rind and anchovy to the pan and cook for 30 seconds, mashing the anchovy lightly so it dissolves into the sauce. Pour in the wine and leave to simmer for a couple of minutes. Add the chilli flakes, tomatoes and clams to the pan. Cover with a lid and leave for 5 minutes until the clams have opened, discarding any that do not open. Add a tablespoon of lemon juice to the pan and season with pepper.

· Meanwhile, heat a large pan of lightly salted water until boiling and then add the spaghetti. Cook according to the pack instructions, drain, reserving a little of the cooking water, and return to the pan.

· Stir through the clams and any juices with a little cooking water to loosen if necessary, then toss through the rocket just before serving.

2 Clam and Tomato Soup with Rocket Dressing

Heat 2 tablespoons olive oil in a pan, add 1 chopped onion and cook for 5 minutes until softened. Add 2 finely chopped garlic cloves and cook for 30 seconds more. Pour over 200 g (7 oz) can tomatoes and 1.2 litres (2 pints) chicken or vegetable stock. Leave to simmer for 5 minutes. Add 300 g (10 oz) clams and cook for 5 minutes, discarding any that do not open. Meanwhile, whizz together 75 g (3 oz) rocket leaves with 4 tablespoons olive oil. Swirl over the soup before serving.

3 Tomato Baked Clams

Heat 100 ml (3½ fl oz) dry white wine in a pan. Add 450 g (14½ oz) clams, cover and steam for 5 minutes. Discard any that do not open and leave to cool for a couple of minutes. Reserve the cooking liquid. Remove the meat from the clams and set aside. Break apart the clam shells and place 12 of the most attractive halves on a baking sheet. Heat 2 tablespoons olive oil in a pan, add 1 finely chopped shallot and cook for 3 minutes. Stir in 1 crushed garlic clove, then add 2 chopped tomatoes. Pour over the clam cooking liquid and cook for 5 minutes until the liquid has boiled away. Stir in the clam meat, a squeeze of lemon juice, a handful of finely chopped rocket and 125 g (4 oz) fresh breadcrumbs. Spoon the mixture into the clam shells and drizzle with a little more oil. Cook under a hot grill for 3–5 minutes until golden and crisp.

Salmon Carpaccio with Beetroot Topping

Serves 4

500 g (1 lb) piece of really fresh
  skinless, boneless salmon
100 ml (3½ fl oz) crème fraîche
1–2 tablespoons horseradish
  sauce
squeeze of lemon juice
finely grated rind of ½ orange
1 tablespoon olive oil
75 g (3 oz) salad leaves
125 g (4 oz) cooked beetroot (not
  preserved in vinegar), chopped
salt and pepper

- Trim any brown flesh from the salmon and slice it thinly. Place the slices between 2 pieces of clingfilm, leaving plenty of space between, then use a mallet or rolling pin to pound the salmon gently until it is thin but not mushy.

- Mix together the crème fraîche and horseradish to taste. Arrange the salmon slices on plates.

- Toss together the lemon juice, orange rind and olive oil with the salad leaves and beetroot and season to taste. Arrange the salad on top of the salmon and drizzle over the crème fraîche to serve.

 Smoked Salmon Bites with Beetroot Salad Mix together 75 ml (3 fl oz) crème fraîche with 1 tablespoon horseradish sauce. Arrange 4 slices of smoked salmon in little nest shapes in the middles of 4 serving plates. Place a little of the horseradish inside each. Whisk together 1 tablespoon red wine vinegar with 3 tablespoons olive oil and mix with 150 g (5 oz) salad leaves. Add 125 g (4 oz) chopped, cooked beetroot. Arrange around the salmon and sprinkle over black pepper and snipped dill before serving.

 Smoked Salmon and Beetroot Bites Line 4 individual ramekins with clingfilm. Carefully place a large slice of smoked salmon in each ramekin, draping the ends over the sides of the ramekins. Roughly chop 200 g (7 oz) smoked salmon and mix together with 1 small chopped beetroot. Stir in 2 tablespoons crème fraîche, the finely grated rind of ½ lemon and 1 tablespoon lemon juice. Fill the ramekins with the mixture, folding the salmon slices over the top so the filling is completely enclosed. Place in the refrigerator to firm for 15–20 minutes. Turn each salmon bite out on to a plate and serve with a crisp green salad.

Blue Cheese Soufflé with Apple and Rocket

Serves 6

75 g (3 oz) crustless sourdough bread, cut into chunks

250 ml (8 fl oz) milk

150 g (5 oz) blue cheese

50 g (2 oz) butter, softened, plus extra for greasing

4 eggs, separated

1 tablespoon white wine vinegar

3 tablespoons olive oil

1 teaspoon walnut oil

1 red apple, cored and thinly sliced

handful of rocket leaves

salt and pepper

- Put the bread in a bowl and pour over the milk. Leave for 5 minutes, then squeeze any excess milk from the bread. Transfer the bread to a food processor with the cheese, butter and egg yolks and process until smooth. Season to taste. Whisk the egg whites until stiff peaks form. Stir a large spoonful into the cheese mixture, then carefully fold in the remainder, half at a time.

- Spoon the mixture into 6 well-buttered ramekins, each holding 150 ml (¼ pint), and bake in a preheated oven, 220°C (425°F), Gas Mark 7, for 10–15 minutes until puffed and golden.

- Meanwhile, whisk together the white wine vinegar, olive oil and walnut oil and season to taste. Toss together with the apple and rocket leaves and serve alongside the soufflés.

 Blue Cheese Waldorf Salad Mash 75 g (3 oz) blue cheese together with 6 tablespoons mayonnaise. Stir together with 3 chopped apples, 6 chopped celery sticks, 2 sliced spring onions and 50 g (2 oz) toasted chopped walnuts. Place in a serving dish and scatter over some more walnuts, blue cheese and celery leaves to serve.

 Baked Mushrooms with Blue Cheese Soufflé Topping Put 6 field mushrooms on a baking sheet. Stir together 175 g (6 oz) blue cheese and 5 tablespoons crème fraîche until smooth, then mix in 3 egg yolks and a handful of finely chopped thyme. Whisk 3 egg whites until stiff peaks form. Carefully fold into the cheese mixture. Spoon a little of the mixture on top of each mushroom and cook in a preheated oven, 220°C (425°F), Gas Mark 7, for 12 minutes or until golden and puffed.

Caesar Salad

Serves 4

½ baguette, torn into chunks

2 tablespoons olive oil

12 quails' eggs

1 garlic clove, crushed

2 canned anchovy fillets, very finely chopped

2 tablespoons crème fraîche

1 teaspoon Dijon mustard

4 tablespoons extra virgin olive oil

25 g (1 oz) Parmesan cheese, grated, plus extra shavings to serve

lemon juice, to taste

2 baby cos (romaine) lettuces, leaves separated

pepper

- Toss the baguette chunks with the olive oil, transfer to a baking sheet and bake in a preheated oven, 200°C (400°F), Gas Mark 6, for 7–10 minutes until golden and crisp. Leave to cool. Carefully lower the eggs into a pan of boiling water and cook for 5 minutes, then cool under cold running water. Shell and halve.

- Mix together the garlic, anchovies, crème fraîche and mustard, then slowly whisk in the olive oil. Stir through the grated Parmesan, season with pepper and stir in lemon juice to taste.

- Arrange the salad leaves on plates along with the baguette chunks and eggs. Drizzle over the sauce and scatter over the Parmesan shavings to serve.

 Open Chicken Caesar Sandwich

Mash 1 canned anchovy fillet and mix together with 4 tablespoons mayonnaise, a handful of grated Parmesan and 1 tablespoon lemon juice. Spread over 4 slices of lightly toasted bread and top with 1 baby cos lettuce, roughly chopped. Place 2 sliced, ready-cooked chicken breasts on top and grate a little more Parmesan over the sandwiches to finish.

 Caesar Salad with Poached Eggs and Fresh Mayonnaise Whisk 2 egg yolks with 1 teaspoon Dijon mustard, 2 finely chopped canned anchovy fillets and 1 crushed garlic clove. Slowly whisk in 300 ml (½ pint) olive oil, a drop at a time to start with. When the mixture is thick and creamy, stir in 3 tablespoons crème fraîche and 25 g (1 oz) grated Parmesan. Season to taste with lemon juice and salt and pepper. Cut ½ sourdough loaf into slices, brush with olive oil and cook on a smoking hot griddle pan for 2–3 minutes on each side until charred and

lightly crisp. Heat a pan of water and 1 tablespoon white wine vinegar until boiling. Reduce the heat to a low simmer and make a whirlpool in the centre of the pan by stirring vigorously with a spoon. Crack an egg into a cup and slip it into the middle of the whirlpool. Cook for 4 minutes and remove with a slotted spoon. Repeat to poach 4 eggs. Toss 2 sliced cos lettuces with the dressing and arrange on plates with the bread, cut into chunks. Return the eggs to the pan for 30 seconds to reheat and serve on top of the salad sprinkled with grated Parmesan.

2 ⟋ Baked Feta with Watermelon

Serves 4

200 g (7 oz) feta cheese
5 tablespoons extra virgin olive oil
250 g (8 oz) watermelon, sliced
75 g (3 oz) pitted Kalamata olives, chopped
pinch of dried chilli flakes
handful of mint leaves

- Tear off a large sheet of kitchen foil. Place the feta on the foil and drizzle over 1 tablespoon of oil. Fold over the edges of the foil to enclose, transfer to a baking sheet and cook in a preheated oven, 190°C (375°F), Gas Mark 5, for 12 minutes.

- Arrange the remaining ingredients on serving plates, crumble the warm feta on top, then drizzle with the remaining oil.

---

1 ⟋ Watermelon and Feta Salad

Whisk together 1 tablespoon white wine vinegar with 3 tablespoons extra virgin olive oil and a pinch of chilli flakes. Toss together with 2 chopped tomatoes, 250 g (8 oz) chopped watermelon and a handful of watercress leaves and arrange on 4 serving plates. Scatter over 150 g (5 oz) crumbled feta cheese to serve.

3 ⟋ Feta Bites with Watermelon Salsa

Stir together 200 g (7 oz) crumbled feta cheese with 125 g (4 oz) mascarpone cheese and 1 tablespoon beaten egg. Cut 4 sheets of filo pastry in half to make 8 squares. Cover the pastry with a damp but not wet sheet of kitchen paper. Lay one sheet in front of you and spoon a little of the feta mixture on one end. Brush around the edges with beaten egg. Fold in the 2 long sides, then tightly roll up the parcel, making sure it is completely enclosed. Repeat with the remaining rolls. Heat a large, deep pan one-third full of oil until a piece of bread crisps and browns in 15 seconds. Cook the rolls, in batches, for 2–3 minutes until golden and crisp and keep warm. Finely chop 150 g (5 oz) watermelon and mix with 1 finely chopped chilli, 1 tablespoon finely chopped red onion and a large handful of chopped mint. Serve in a bowl alongside the feta bites.

Red Pepper Dip with Herb Pitta Crackers

Serves 4

5 tablespoons olive oil
1 shallot, finely chopped
100 g (3½ oz) walnut halves
200 g (7 oz) ready-roasted red peppers
1 garlic clove, crushed
1 teaspoon ground cumin
1 tablespoon pomegranate molasses
4 pitta breads
handful of chopped parsley
handful of chopped mint
coarse sea salt

- Heat 1 tablespoon oil in a frying pan, add the shallot and cook for 3 minutes until softened. Leave to cool. Toast the walnut halves in a dry frying pan for 3 minutes until lightly browned and leave to cool. Put the walnuts in a blender with the shallot, peppers, garlic, cumin, pomegranate molasses and 2 tablespoons oil and whizz together until smooth. Season to taste.

- Meanwhile, split the pittas open horizontally and cut each half into wedges. Mix together the remaining oil with the herbs and brush over the wedges. Place on a baking sheet, sprinkle with coarse sea salt and bake in a preheated oven, 190°C (375°F), Gas Mark 5, for 5–7 minutes or until golden and crisp. Serve alongside the red pepper dip.

Herb and Roasted Pepper Salad

Lightly toast 25 g (1 oz) walnut halves in a dry frying pan. Whisk 1 tablespoon sherry vinegar with 3 tablespoons olive oil. Toss with 150 g (5 oz) mixed herb salad and 2 ready-roasted red peppers, cut into strips. Season to taste. Arrange on a plate, then scatter over the walnuts and 50 g (2 oz) crumbled soft goats' cheese.

Herby Couscous Stuffed Peppers

Put 75 g (3 oz) couscous in a bowl, pour over 100 ml (3½ fl oz) hot vegetable stock, cover and leave for 5 minutes until soft. Stir through 3 tablespoons olive oil, 2 chopped tomatoes, 1 teaspoon balsamic vinegar and a large handful each of chopped mint and parsley. Season to taste. Meanwhile, halve 2 red peppers lengthways and remove the cores and seeds. Place the peppers on a baking sheet and spoon the couscous mixture into the cavities. Drizzle over 1 tablespoon olive oil and cook in a preheated oven, 200°C (400°F), Gas Mark 6, for 20–25 minutes or until the peppers are just soft.

Spiced Mussels in a Coconut Broth

Serves 4

1 tablespoon vegetable oil
1 shallot, finely chopped
1 garlic clove, sliced
1 red chilli, chopped
2 lime leaves, shredded
125 ml (4 fl oz) coconut milk
125 ml (4 fl oz) water
1 lemon grass stalk
1 tablespoon Thai fish sauce
1 tablespoon soft brown sugar
1 kg (2 lb) mussels, scrubbed
handful of fresh coriander,
   chopped

- Heat the oil in a large saucepan, add the shallot and cook for 2 minutes. Stir in the garlic, chilli and lime leaves and cook for 1 minute more. Pour in the coconut milk and the measurement water, add the lemon grass, fish sauce and sugar and leave to simmer for 10 minutes.

- Add the mussels, cover and cook for 3–5 minutes until the mussels are open, discarding any that do not open. Scatter over the coriander to serve.

 Spicy Wok-Roasted Mussels

Heat 1 tablespoon vegetable oil in a large wok, add 1 tablespoon Thai green curry paste and cook for 1 minute. Add 1 kg (2 lb) cleaned mussels and cook for 1 minute. Pour over 50 ml (2 fl oz) coconut milk, cover and cook for 2 minutes more until the mussels are open, discarding any that do not open. Scatter over 1 chopped spring onion, a handful of chopped fresh coriander and 1 tablespoon lime juice to serve.

Seafood Laksa

Heat 1 tablespoon vegetable oil in a large saucepan, add 1 tablespoon Thai red curry paste and a pinch of turmeric and cook for 1 minute. Add 400 ml (14 fl oz) can coconut milk, 1.5 cm (¾ inch) piece of fresh root ginger, 2 lime leaves and 600 ml (1 pint) chicken stock. Bring to the boil, reduce the heat and leave to simmer for 15 minutes. Remove the ginger and lime leaves. Add 150 g (5 oz) large raw peeled prawns and 500 g (1 lb) cleaned mussels and cook for 3 minutes until just cooked through. Remove any mussels that do not open. Meanwhile, cook 150 g (5 oz) rice noodles according to the pack instructions. Add to the soup along with 75 g (3 oz) squid cut into rings and leave for 1 minute until the squid is cooked through. Serve sprinkled with a handful of bean sprouts and some chopped mint and coriander leaves.

30 Chicken Liver Pâté

Serves 6

1 tablespoon olive oil
1 shallot, finely chopped
250 g (8 oz) chicken livers
100 ml (3½ fl oz) vin santo or
 other dessert wine
250 ml (8 fl oz) double cream
½ baguette, thinly sliced
salt and pepper

To serve

red onion, finely chopped
capers

- Heat the oil in a frying pan, add the shallot and cook for 3 minutes until softened. Wash the chicken livers and trim away any sinews. Pat dry and add to the pan. Season to taste and cook until browned all over but still soft to the touch. Pour in the wine and cook for 5 minutes. Add the cream and cook for a further 5–10 minutes until reduced by half. Whizz in a food processor until smooth, then check and adjust the seasoning if necessary. If you want it extra smooth, press the mixture through a sieve. Transfer to a serving bowl and leave to cool to room temperature.

- Meanwhile, toast the baguette slices until golden and crisp and leave to cool. Serve alongside the pâté with some finely chopped red onion and capers for scattering over, if liked.

1 Seared Liver Toasts with

Creamy Marsala Sauce Heat 2 tablespoons olive oil in a heavy-based pan and add 400 g (13 oz) trimmed and cleaned chicken livers and 1 sliced shallot. Cook for 5 minutes until golden all over. Pour over 75 ml (3 fl oz) Marsala and leave to cook for 3 minutes until reduced down. Stir in 3 tablespoons double cream, season to taste and warm through. Lightly toast 6 slices of brioche. Spoon the livers and sauce over the toast, sprinkle with chopped parsley and serve.

2 Chopped Chicken Liver and Eggs

Heat 1 tablespoon oil in a pan, add 1 chopped onion and cook over a low heat for 10 minutes until soft. Heat another tablespoon of oil in a frying pan and cook 400 g (13 oz) trimmed chicken livers for 8 minutes until golden and just cooked through. Leave to cool. Put the onion and liver in a food processor and pulse to make a coarse purée. Stir in 4 chopped hard-boiled eggs and season to taste. Cool and serve with toasted challah bread or crackers.

 # Broad Bean and Pea Crostini

Serves 6

75 ml (3 fl oz) olive oil
1 lemon
2 garlic cloves, peeled
300 g (10 oz) broad beans
300 g (10 oz) peas
6 slices of sourdough bread
handful of mint leaves
salt and pepper

To serve

2 radishes, thinly sliced
handful of pea shoots
Pecorino cheese shavings

- Put the oil, 3 strips of lemon rind and the garlic cloves in a small pan and cook over a very low heat for 7–10 minutes. Remove from the heat and discard the lemon rind.

- Cook the broad beans and peas in a pan of lightly salted boiling water for 3 minutes until just soft. Drain and rinse under cold running water to cool. Peel the broad beans.

- Tip most of the peas and beans into a blender, add the mint and cooked garlic together with the flavoured oil and pulse to make a rough purée. Season well.

- Toast the bread, halve the slices and arrange on a serving platter. Spread with the purée and scatter with the reserved peas and broad beans. Top with radishes, pea shoots and Pecorino cheese shavings and serve.

---

1 ◔ Pea and Broad Bean Salad

Cook 100 g (3½ oz) each of peas and broad beans in lightly salted boiling water for 3 minutes until soft, drain and cool under cold running water. Whisk 3 tablespoons olive oil with 1 tablespoon lemon juice, season and toss with 150 g (5 oz) salad leaves. Place on serving plates, scatter over the peas and beans and top with Pecorino cheese shavings to serve.

3 ◑ Pea and Broad Bean Soup

Heat 1 tablespoon olive oil in a pan, add 1 finely chopped onion and cook for 5 minutes until softened. Add 75 g (3 oz) lardons and cook for 5 minutes more until browned. Stir in 1 crushed garlic clove and cook for 1 minute until soft. Stir in 1 tablespoon plain flour and cook for 2 minutes, then stir in 75 ml (3 fl oz) dry white wine. Cook for 5 minutes until reduced, then pour over 1.5 litres (2½ pints) chicken or vegetable stock and leave to simmer for 10 minutes. Stir in 150 g (5 oz) fine asparagus tips and 200 g (7 oz) each of peas and broad beans and cook for 3 minutes until soft. Divide the soup between 6 bowls, scatter over a handful of mint leaves and some Pecorino shavings and serve with toasted sourdough bread.

QuickCook
Meat and Poultry

Recipes listed by cooking time

30

20

10

Roasted Chicken Breasts with Herb Butter

Serves 4

50 g (2 oz) butter, softened
grated rind of 1 lemon
1 garlic clove, crushed
handful of basil, finely chopped
4 skinless, boneless chicken
   breasts
6 tablespoons olive oil, plus extra
   for greasing
100 g (3½ oz) dry breadcrumbs
25 g (1 oz) Parmesan cheese,
   grated
salt and pepper

To serve

new potatoes
green beans

- Mix together the butter, lemon rind, garlic and basil and season to taste. Use a sharp knife to make a small horizontal slit in the side of each chicken breast to form a little pocket, making sure you don't cut all the way through the meat. Tuck some of the butter inside each breast, then smooth over to seal.

- Rub 1 tablespoon oil over each chicken breast and season well. Put the breadcrumbs on a plate and dip each breast in the crumbs until well coated.

- Transfer the chicken to a lightly greased baking tin, sprinkle over the Parmesan, drizzle with the remaining oil and cook in a preheated oven, 200°C (400°F), Gas Mark 6, for 15 minutes or until golden and cooked through. Serve with new potatoes and green beans.

---

1 Herby Chicken Sandwiches

Mix together 6 tablespoons mayonnaise, the finely grated rind of ½ lemon and a handful of chopped basil. Cut 4 chicken breasts into slices, season and rub with 2 tablespoons oil. Cook on a preheated griddle pan for 5 minutes, turning once, until seared and cooked through. Spread the mayonnaise on the cut sides of 4 split ciabatta rolls and fill with the warm chicken and some salad leaves.

3 Herb Butter Chicken Kievs

Mix together 50 g (2 oz) softened butter, the grated rind of 1 lemon, 1 crushed garlic clove and a handful of finely chopped basil. Season to taste and use to fill 4 skinless, boneless chicken breasts as in the first step of the main recipe. Sprinkle 50 g (2 oz) flour on a plate. Pour 1 lightly beaten egg on to a second plate and spread 100 g (3½ oz) breadcrumbs on a third. Dip the chicken in the flour, dusting off any excess, then in the egg and finally in the breadcrumbs. Heat a large frying pan and add 6 tablespoons vegetable oil. Cook the chicken for 3 minutes on each side until golden. Remove from the pan and pat with kitchen paper. Place on a baking sheet and cook in a preheated oven, 180°C (350°F), Gas Mark 4, for 15–20 minutes until cooked through. Serve with a green salad and chips.

 # Chicken, Leek and Tarragon Pie

Serves 4

2 leeks, cut into thin rounds

8 ready-roasted chicken legs, bones removed and meat roughly chopped

125 g (4 oz) thick piece of ham, cubed

150 ml (5 fl oz) crème fraîche

handful of tarragon leaves, chopped

375 g (12 oz) ready-rolled shortcrust pastry

1 egg, lightly beaten

salt and pepper

To serve

peas

mashed potatoes

- Put the leeks in a sieve or colander and pour over a kettleful of boiling water until starting to wilt. Mix the leeks together with the chicken meat, ham, crème fraîche and tarragon and season. Transfer the mixture to a 23 cm (9 inch) pie dish.

- Place the pastry on top, crimp around the edges and cut away any excess pastry. Make a small slit in the centre of the pastry and brush all over with the egg. Cook in a preheated oven, 220°C (425°F), Gas Mark 7, for 20–25 minutes until golden and bubbling. Serve with peas and mashed potatoes.

 ## Chicken, Tarragon and Bacon Salad

Cook 4 streaky bacon rashers under a preheated hot grill for 7 minutes, turning once, until crisp. Mix 200 ml (7 fl oz) natural yogurt, 4 tablespoons mayonnaise, 1 tablespoon wholegrain mustard and a handful of chopped tarragon and season to taste. Combine with 3 sliced ready-roasted chicken breasts. Toss the leaves from 1 lettuce and 1 head of chicory with 3 tablespoons olive oil and 1 tablespoon white wine vinegar. Arrange on a plate with 75 g (3 oz) sliced radishes. Top with the chicken and crumble over the bacon to serve.

 ## Seared Chicken in Tarragon Bacon

Sauce Heat 1 tablespoon oil in a large frying pan. Add 4 skinless, boneless chicken breasts, season and cook for 7 minutes. Turn over and cook for 5 minutes more or until golden and cooked through. Remove from the pan and keep warm. Add 50 g (2 oz) lardons and 1 finely chopped shallot and cook for 3 minutes until softened. Pour in 100 ml (3½ fl oz) dry white wine. Boil for a few minutes until reduced by half, then whisk in 50 g (2 oz) cold butter cut into cubes to form a sauce. Add 1 tablespoon lemon juice and a handful of chopped tarragon, then spoon over the chicken. Serve with green beans and mashed potatoes.

2 🕐 Saffron Roasted Chicken

Serves 4

3 tablespoons milk
pinch of saffron threads
75 ml (3 fl oz) natural yogurt
2 garlic cloves, crushed
2 teaspoons finely grated fresh
  root ginger
25 g (1 oz) ground almonds
2 teaspoons toasted cumin seeds
4 chicken breasts
15 g (½ oz) butter, plus extra for
  greasing
25 g (1 oz) flaked almonds
handful of mint leaves
1 green chilli, deseeded and
  chopped
salt and pepper

To serve

tomato salad
plain boiled rice

- Heat the milk, add the saffron and set aside. Mix together the yogurt, garlic, ginger, ground almonds and cumin seeds and season well. Coat the chicken in the mixture, place on a lightly greased baking sheet and cook in a preheated oven, 220°C (425°F), Gas Mark 7, for 10 minutes.

- Pour over the saffron liquid, dot with the butter and scatter over the flaked almonds, then cook for 5 minutes more or until the chicken is cooked through. Sprinkle over the mint leaves and chilli and serve with a tomato salad and boiled rice.

---

1 🕐 Chicken Chapatti Wraps

Mix 300 g (10 oz) chicken stir-fry strips with 25 g (1 oz) natural yogurt, a pinch of saffron threads, 1 teaspoon ground cumin and a pinch of dried chilli flakes. Season to taste and drizzle over 1 tablespoon oil. Heat a griddle pan until smoking and cook the chicken for 3–4 minutes on each side until cooked through. Place on 4 warmed chapattis and top with chopped tomatoes, sliced Little Gem lettuce leaves and some chopped fresh coriander.

3 🕐 Saffron Chicken Pilaff

Heat 1 tablespoon oil in a frying pan, add 4 boneless chicken thighs cut into chunks and cook for 5–7 minutes until golden all over. Melt 25 g (1 oz) butter in a large saucepan, add 1 tablespoon oil and cook 1 finely chopped onion for 5 minutes. Add 2 finely chopped garlic cloves, 2 teaspoons grated fresh root ginger, 2 teaspoons cumin seeds and 1 teaspoon coriander seeds and cook for 1 minute. Stir in 300 g (10 oz) basmati rice and a pinch of saffron threads. Return the chicken to the pan, then pour over 900 ml (1½ pints) chicken stock. Season to taste, bring to the boil and cook for 10 minutes. Lower the heat, cover the pan and cook for a further 5 minutes until the chicken is cooked through and the rice is tender. Grate ½ cucumber and mix with the finely grated rind of 1 lime, 1 tablespoon lime juice, 1 crushed garlic clove and 100 ml (3½ fl oz) natural yogurt. Season to taste, stir in chopped mint leaves and serve with the pilaff.

 # Chicken and Chermoula Pilaff

Serves 6

4 tablespoons olive oil
finely grated rind and juice of
   1 lemon
2 teaspoons ground cumin
large handful of fresh coriander,
   chopped
large handful of parsley, chopped
6 small chicken breasts, thickly
   sliced
1 onion, finely chopped
1 garlic clove, crushed
300 g (10 oz) bulgar wheat
500 ml (17 fl oz) hot chicken
   stock
1 tablespoon pomegranate
   molasses
seeds from 1 pomegranate
salt and pepper

- Mix together 2 tablespoons olive oil with half the grated lemon rind and juice, 1 teaspoon cumin, and a little coriander and parsley. Rub all over the chicken and leave to marinate for 5–10 minutes.

- Heat 1 tablespoon oil in a large pan. Add the onion and cook for 5 minutes until softened. Stir in the garlic and cook for 30 seconds. Add the remaining cumin, then stir in the bulgar wheat and cook for 1 minute. Pour over the stock, cover and leave to simmer for 15 minutes or until all the liquid has been absorbed.

- Meanwhile, heat a small frying pan and toast the walnuts for 3–5 minutes, then remove from the pan and set aside. Heat a griddle pan until smoking, add the chicken and cook for 3–5 minutes on each side until charred and cooked through. Mix together the remaining oil, the pomegranate molasses and the remaining lemon juice and rind. Toss through the bulgar wheat along with the chicken, pomegranate seeds and the remaining herbs.

---

1 **Chicken Couscous Salad**

Put 375 g (12 oz) couscous into a bowl. Pour over 500 ml (17 fl oz) hot chicken stock, cover and leave for 5 minutes. Fluff the grains with a fork, then add 4 ready-roasted chicken breasts, torn into strips, 3 tablespoons olive oil, the juice and finely grated rind of 1 lemon, 200 g (7 oz) can rinsed and drained chickpeas, 50 g (2 oz) chopped olives and a large handful of chopped fresh coriander.

2 **Chicken Tagine with Bulgar Wheat**

Heat 2 tablespoons olive oil in a large casserole. Cook 6 skinless, boneless chicken breasts for 2–3 minutes on each side until golden, then remove from the pan. Add 1 finely chopped onion and cook for 5 minutes until softened. Stir in 1 crushed garlic clove, 2 teaspoons ground cumin, ½ finely chopped green chilli, a pinch of saffron threads and a large handful each of chopped fresh coriander

and parsley. Add the juice and finely grated rind of 1 lemon and 125 ml (4 fl oz) water and simmer for 2 minutes. Return the chicken to the pan and cook for 5–10 minutes until cooked through. Serve with steamed bulgar wheat.

Spicy Stir-Fried Chilli Chicken

Serves 4

400 g (13 oz) chicken breast,
  sliced
3 tablespoons light soy sauce
3 tablespoons rice wine
1 tablespoon cornflour
3 tablespoons vegetable oil
75 g (3 oz) cashew nuts
2 spring onions, sliced
3 garlic cloves, sliced
1 tablespoon grated fresh
  root ginger
1 teaspoon chilli sauce
2 teaspoons caster sugar
3–4 tablespoons water

To serve

boiled rice
wilted watercress

- Mix together the chicken with 1 tablespoon each soy sauce and rice wine and 1 teaspoon cornflour. Leave to marinate for 5–10 minutes.

- Heat 1 tablespoon oil in a wok or large frying pan, add the cashew nuts and stir around the pan for 2 minutes until lightly browned, then remove from the pan. Heat the remaining oil and cook the chicken for 5–7 minutes until just cooked through. Remove from the pan.

- Add the spring onions, garlic and ginger and cook for 30 seconds, then return the chicken and nuts to the pan, stir in the remaining soy sauce, rice wine and cornflour, the chilli sauce, caster sugar and measurement water. Heat until bubbling and slightly thickened. Serve with boiled rice and wilted watercress.

Chilli Chicken Skewers

Cut 2 large chicken breasts into long thin strips and thread on to metal skewers. Mix together 1 tablespoon each chilli sauce and vegetable oil with 2 tablespoons soy sauce and rub over the chicken. Cook on a smoking griddle pan for 3–4 minutes on each side until just cooked through. Serve with ready-cooked rice noodles tossed together with 2 tablespoons each soy sauce and rice wine and ¼ cucumber, thinly sliced.

Lemon Chilli Pilaff with Seared

Chicken Heat 2 tablespoons oil in a large saucepan, add 1 finely chopped onion and cook for 5 minutes until softened. Add 2 finely chopped garlic cloves and 2 teaspoons grated fresh roor ginger and cook for 30 seconds. Stir in ½ deseeded and chopped chilli, the finely grated rind of 1 lemon and 300 g (10 oz) basmati rice. Pour over 650 ml (23 fl oz) chicken stock and season to taste. Leave to bubble for 10 minutes, then reduce the heat to low, cover and cook for 5 minutes until the rice is soft. Stir in 25 g (1 oz) toasted cashew nuts. Meanwhile, cut 1 red pepper into strips and toss with 8 boneless, skinless chicken thighs, 2 tablespoons soy sauce, 1 tablespoon vegetable oil and 2 tablespoons lemon juice. Heat a griddle pan until smoking and cook the chicken for 5 minutes, turn over, add the peppers and cook for a further 5–7 minutes, until charred and cooked through. Serve the chicken with the pilaff.

1 Chicken Saltimbocca

Serves 4

4 chicken breasts
8 slices of prosciutto
8 sage leaves

To serve

green beans
new potatoes

- Use a sharp knife to slice each chicken breast in half horizontally to make 8 thin pieces. Place the chicken on a greased baking sheet and cook under a preheated hot grill for 2 minutes.

- Turn the chicken over and drape a slice of prosciutto over each piece. Return to the grill for a further 2 minutes until the prosciutto begins to crisp. Place a sage leaf on top of each and cook for a further 1 minute until the chicken is cooked through and the prosciutto and sage are crisp. Serve with green beans and new potatoes.

2 Parma Ham Roasted Chicken

Use a sharp knife to make a small horizontal slit in the sides of 4 chicken breasts to form a little pocket, making sure you don't cut all the way through the meat. Mix 5 tablespoons cream cheese with a handful of chopped basil and the finely grated rind of ½ lemon. Season and stuff a little of the mixture inside each pocket. Smooth over to seal, then wrap a piece of Parma ham around each one. Place on a lightly greased baking sheet and cook in a preheated oven, 220°C (425°F), Gas Mark 7, for 10 minutes. Add 150 g (5 oz) cherry tomatoes, drizzle over 1 tablespoon olive oil and cook for a further 5 minutes or until the chicken is cooked through.

3 Chicken and Bacon Stew

Cut 4 chicken thighs into large chunks. Heat 1 tablespoon vegetable oil in a large frying pan and cook the chicken for 5–7 minutes until golden. Meanwhile, heat 1 tablespoon vegetable oil in a casserole, then add 1 chopped onion and 4 chopped streaky bacon rashers. Cook for 5 minutes until softened. Pour over 125 ml (4 fl oz) dry white wine and boil until reduced by half. Add the chicken to the casserole along with 2 thyme sprigs and 150 ml (¼ pint) chicken stock. Simmer for 15 minutes until the chicken is cooked through. Heat 1 tablespoon oil in the frying pan, then add 150 g (5 oz) sliced wild mushrooms and cook for 3–5 minutes until soft and lightly browned. Stir the mushrooms into the stew along with 3 tablespoons crème fraîche. Serve with mashed potatoes scattered with a handful of chopped parsley.

FOO-MEAT-NOO

1 Smoked Duck, Orange and Watercress Salad

Serves 4

2 large oranges
1 tablespoon rice wine vinegar
3 tablespoons vegetable oil
150 g (5 oz) watercress
1 head of chicory
1 spring onion, sliced
150 g (5 oz) radishes, sliced
250 g (8 oz) sliced smoked
　duck breast
salt and pepper

- Cut the peel from the oranges using a sharp knife. Divide the oranges into segments by cutting between the membranes, holding them over a bowl to catch the juice. Mix the juice with the rice wine vinegar and oil and season well.

- Toss the dressing with the watercress, chicory leaves and spring onion. Arrange the salad on serving plates with the orange segments, radishes and smoked duck.

2 Seared Duck with Citrus Salad

Rub 1 teaspoon five spice powder over 4 duck breasts. Heat a nonstick frying pan and cook the duck, skin side down, for 5 minutes. Turn over and cook for 3–5 minutes more until cooked to your liking. Cut 1 carrot into batons and cook in a saucepan of lightly salted boiling water with 100 g (3½ oz) sugarsnap peas for 3 minutes or until just cooked through. Drain and cool under cold running water. Whisk together 2 teaspoons finely grated fresh root ginger, 2 teaspoons soy sauce, 3 tablespoons lime juice, 1 tablespoon orange juice, 1 tablespoon clear honey and 3 tablespoons vegetable oil. Toss together with the cooked vegetables, 150 g (5 oz)

shredded Chinese cabbage, 50 g (2 oz) bean sprouts and a large handful of fresh coriander leaves. Cut the duck into slices and serve alongside the salad.

3 Smoked Duck Risotto with Watercress

Heat 25 g (1 oz) butter and 1 tablespoon olive oil in a pan. Add 1 finely chopped shallot and cook for 5 minutes until softened. Stir in 300 g (10 oz) risotto rice and 1 teaspoon finely grated orange rind, then add 125 ml (4 fl oz) dry white wine. Cook until bubbled away, then gradually stir in 900 ml (1½ pints) hot chicken stock, a little at a time, stirring frequently, allowing the rice to absorb the stock before adding more. When the rice is soft, after about 15 minutes, add 100 g (3½ oz) frozen peas and 125 g (4 oz) chopped watercress. Cook until wilted, then add 50 g (2 oz) grated Parmesan and season to taste. Top with 150 g (5 oz) sliced smoked duck breast to serve.

 # Mustard Rarebit-Style Pork Chops

Serves 4

4 pork chops
oil, for greasing
50 g (2 oz) Cheddar cheese, grated
2 tablespoons crème fraîche
1 tablespoon wholegrain mustard
salt and pepper

To serve

green beans
new potatoes

- Put the pork chops on a lightly greased baking sheet, season to taste and cook in a preheated oven, 200°C (400°F), Gas Mark 6, for 15 minutes.

- Mix together the cheese, crème fraîche and mustard. Spread a little over the top of each pork chop and return to the oven for 2 minutes or until the topping has just melted. Serve with new potatoes and green beans.

 Creamy Bacon and Mustard Pasta

Heat 1 tablespoon olive oil in a frying pan. Cut 6 streaky bacon rashers into thin slices, add to the pan and cook for 5–7 minutes until browned and crispy. Cook 500 g (1 lb) fresh penne pasta in a large saucepan of lightly salted boiling water according to the pack instructions. Drain and stir in 1 tablespoon wholegrain mustard, the finely grated rind of 1 lemon and 4 tablespoons crème fraîche. Add the bacon, season to taste and sprinkle with chopped parsley to serve.

 Crispy Mustard Pork Tenderloin

Pat dry 2 pork tenderloins, then dust with plain flour. Brush 2 tablespoons Dijon mustard over the pork and season. Spread 125 g (4 oz) dry breadcrumbs on a plate with a handful of chopped thyme and 50 g (2 oz) grated Parmesan cheese. Roll the tenderloins in this mixture until well coated. Place on a lightly greased baking sheet and drizzle over 2 tablespoons olive oil. Bake in a preheated oven, 220°C (425°F), Gas Mark 7, for 25 minutes until golden and cooked through. Serve with baby new potatoes and green vegetables.

10 Grilled Chorizo with Clam Sauce

Serves 4

4 large cooked chorizo sausages, halved lengthways
3 tablespoons olive oil
1 shallot, finely chopped
1 garlic clove, finely chopped
250 g (8 oz) clams, scrubbed
75 ml (3 fl oz) water
8 slices ciabatta bread, toasted
125 g (4 oz) cherry tomatoes, halved
finely grated rind and juice of 1 lemon
handful of parsley leaves, chopped
rocket leaves, to serve

- Heat a griddle pan until smoking. Add the chorizo and cook for 2 minutes on each side or until lightly charred.

- Meanwhile, heat the olive oil in a large saucepan. Add the shallot and garlic and cook for 3 minutes until softened. Add the clams and the measurement water, cover with a lid and leave for 5 minutes over a low heat until the clams have opened, discarding any that do not open.

- Arrange the toasted ciabatta bread and chorizo in serving bowls. Add the tomatoes, lemon rind and juice and parsley to the pan with the clams and stir until heated through. Spoon the clams over the bread and chorizo and top with rocket leaves.

---

20 Bacon and Clam Tomato Chowder

Heat 1 tablespoon oil in a large saucepan. Add 1 finely chopped onion and 6 chopped streaky bacon rashers. Cook for 5 minutes until the onion is softened. Add 1 litre (1¾ pints) vegetable stock, 400 g (13 oz) can chopped tomatoes and 3 chopped potatoes. Simmer for 10 minutes until the potatoes are beginning to soften, then add 300 g (10 oz) clams. Cover and cook for 5 minutes until the clams have opened, discarding any that do not open. Sprinkle with chopped parsley and serve with crusty bread.

30 Pork Meatballs with Clams

Mix together 2 crushed garlic cloves with 500 g (1 lb) minced pork and 25 g (1 oz) fresh white breadcrumbs and season to taste. Lightly wet your hands and form the mixture into meatballs about the size of a golf ball. Place on a lightly greased baking sheet, drizzle over 1 tablespoon olive oil and cook in a preheated oven, 200°C (400°F), Gas Mark 6, for 20 minutes. Meanwhile, heat 1 tablespoon olive oil in a large saucepan. Add 1 finely chopped onion and cook for 5 minutes until softened, add 1 chopped red pepper and stir through 2 teaspoons tomato purée. Pour over 100 ml (3½ fl oz) dry white wine and allow to bubble until reduced by half. Add 400 g (13 oz) can chopped tomatoes and 1 teaspoon smoked paprika and season to taste. Leave to simmer for 5 minutes, then add the meatballs and 250 g (8 oz) clams. Cover and cook for 5 minutes or until the clams have opened, discarding any that do not open. Sprinkle with chopped parsley before serving.

10 Thai Pork with Mango Salsa

Serves 4

1 lemon grass stalk
2 tablespoons vegetable oil
2 garlic cloves, finely chopped
2 teaspoons chopped fresh
   root ginger
400 g (13 oz) pork stir-fry strips
1 teaspoon caster sugar
2 tablespoons Thai fish sauce
finely grated rind of 1 lime
300 g (10 oz) ready-cooked
   rice noodles
4 Little Gem lettuces
handful of fresh coriander leaves

Salsa

1 mango, peeled, pitted and finely
   chopped
1 spring onion, sliced
1 red chilli, finely chopped
juice of 1 lime
salt and pepper

- Remove the tough outer leaves from the lemon grass and finely shred the core. Heat the oil in a large frying pan or wok, add the garlic and lemon grass and cook for 30 seconds. Stir in the ginger and pork and cook for 5–7 minutes until the pork is just cooked through. Stir the sugar into the fish sauce to dissolve, add the lime rind and stir into the pork. Cook for a further 1 minute until glossy and coated.

- Make the salsa by tossing together all the ingredients and seasoning to taste. Prepare the rice noodles if necessary according to the pack instructions. Mix together the pork, separated lettuce leaves and noodles and divide between 4 serving plates. Scatter over the fresh coriander and top with the mango salsa.

2 Thai Burgers

Roughly grate 1 small onion, squeeze away the juices and mix with 1 tablespoon Thai red curry paste, 1 egg yolk and 500 g (1 lb) minced pork. Add 1 chopped lemon grass stalk, then form into 4 thick burgers. In a smoking hot griddle pan, cook the burgers for 5–7 minutes on each side until just cooked through. Make the salsa as above, then stir in some fresh coriander. Serve the burgers in buns, topped with the salsa.

3 Pork Chops with Mango Ginger Chutney

Heat 1 tablespoon oil in a saucepan, add ½ teaspoon each coriander and cumin seeds and cook for 30 seconds until sizzling. Add 1 finely chopped onion and cook over a low heat for 5–7 minutes until soft and lightly golden. Add 1 cinnamon stick, 2 cardamom pods and a pinch of ground turmeric. Stir in 2 chopped mangoes, ½ finely chopped red chilli, 1 teaspoon finely chopped fresh root ginger, 125 ml (4 fl oz) white wine vinegar, 125 g (4 oz) soft brown sugar and 100 ml (3½ fl oz) water. Leave to simmer for 20 minutes until the mango is soft and the mixture is pulpy. Season to taste. Meanwhile, rub 1 tablespoon oil over 4 pork chops, place under a preheated hot grill and cook for 7 minutes on each side until just cooked through. Serve the chops with a spoonful of the chutney, some green salsa and rice.

20 Pork Chops with Plum Ginger Relish

Serves 4

2 tablespoons olive oil
1 small onion, finely chopped
1 tablespoon grated fresh
   root ginger
4 plums, pitted and sliced
1 tablespoon soft brown sugar
1 teaspoon red wine vinegar
finely grated rind of ½ orange
100 ml (3½ fl oz) water
4 pork chops
handful of watercress, to serve
salt and pepper

- Heat 1 tablespoon oil in a small pan, add the onion and cook for 5 minutes until softened. Add the ginger, plums, sugar, vinegar, orange rind and measurement water and simmer for 10 minutes until soft. Season to taste.

- Meanwhile, rub the remaining oil over the chops and season. Cook under a hot grill for 5 minutes on each side until just cooked through. Serve with spoonfuls of the relish and some watercress.

Grilled Pork with Plum Salsa

Rub 1 tablespoon oil over 4 pork chops. Season and cook under a hot grill for 5 minutes on each side until golden and cooked through. Meanwhile, roughly chop 3 plums and place in a small bowl. Add 1 finely chopped red chilli, the juice of ½ lime, 1 tablespoon orange juice and 2 tablespoons olive oil. Spoon the salsa over the pork chops to serve.

Baked Pork and Plums

Put 4 pork chops in a lightly greased ovenproof dish and arrange 4 halved plums around them. Mix together the juice of 1 orange, 1 teaspoon clear honey, a pinch of dried chilli flakes and 2 teaspoons grated fresh root ginger. Drizzle over the chops, season and bake in a preheated oven, 200°C (400°F), Gas Mark 6, for 20 minutes until browned and the pork is cooked through.

3⦿ Herbed Pork with Creamy Apple Sauce

Serves 6

2 × 500 g (1 lb) pork tenderloins
handful of parsley, chopped
2 teaspoons chopped rosemary
10 slices of pancetta
1 tablespoon oil, plus extra for
greasing
1 onion, chopped
1 apple, cored and cubed
2 tablespoons Calvados or brandy
150 ml (5 fl oz) apple juice
75 ml (3 fl oz) crème fraîche
salt and pepper

To serve

mashed potatoes
watercress

- Use a sharp knife to slice lengthways through each tenderloin (taking care not to cut the whole way through) and then open it out like a book.

- Season the meat and scatter the herbs over the cut sides, then close them again. Lay half the pancetta slices on a sheet of clingfilm and place one piece of pork on top. Bring the clingfilm up and over the pork, so it is wrapped with the pancetta. Repeat with the other tenderloin. Remove the clingfilm, place on a lightly greased baking sheet and cook in a preheated oven, 200°C (400°F), Gas Mark 6, for 20–25 minutes until the meat is cooked through.

- Meanwhile, heat the oil in a frying pan. Add the onion and cook for 5 minutes, then stir in the apple and cook over a medium heat for 3 minutes more until softened and browned. Add the Calvados or brandy to the pan, allow to bubble away, then pour over the apple juice. Cook until reduced by half. Stir in the crème fraîche and season to taste.

- Cut the pork into thick slices and spoon over the sauce. Serve with mashed potatoes and watercress.

1⦿ **Bacon and Apple Salad**

Cook 6 bacon rashers under a hot grill for 3 minutes on each side until just crisp, then cut into slices. Whisk together 1 tablespoon white wine vinegar, 1 teaspoon Dijon mustard and 3 tablespoons olive oil and season. Thinly slice 2 apples and toss with the dressing and 200 g (7 oz) mixed salad leaves. Stir through the bacon and serve.

 2⦿ **Crispy Pork Chops with Apple Slaw**

Lay 6 trimmed pork chops between sheets of clingfilm and flatten with a meat mallet or rolling pin until 1 cm (½ inch) thick. Pour 1 large beaten egg on to a plate. Mix together 150 g (5 oz) dry breadcrumbs with 40 g (1½ oz) grated Parmesan on a plate. Dip the pork into the egg, then the breadcrumbs to coat. Heat 3 tablespoons oil

in a nonstick frying pan and cook the pork for 5–7 minutes on each side until golden and crisp. Meanwhile, finely shred ½ cabbage. Mix the cabbage with 1 apple, cut into matchsticks. Stir 1 teaspoon white wine vinegar together with 100 g (3½ oz) each of mayonnaise and natural yogurt and season. Toss with the apple and cabbage and serve with the pork.

Pork and Pineapple Curry

Serves 4

400 ml (14 fl oz) can coconut milk
2 tablespoons Thai red curry
  paste
2 teaspoons light brown sugar
2 tablespoons Thai fish sauce
2 tablespoons tamarind paste
2 lime leaves
1 tablespoon oil
375 g (12 oz) cubed pork
250 g (8 oz) pineapple, cubed
handful of fresh coriander,
  chopped
50 g (2 oz) bean sprouts
rice, to serve

- Heat a large saucepan. Scoop the thick coconut cream from the top of the can, add it to the pan with the curry paste and cook over a medium heat for 2–3 minutes until really fragrant. Add the remaining coconut milk, the sugar, fish sauce, tamarind paste and lime leaves and simmer for 5 minutes.

- Meanwhile, heat a large frying pan and add the oil. Add the pork and cook for 5 minutes until browned all over. Add the pork to the curry, stir in the pineapple and cook for 10 minutes more. Scatter over the coriander and bean sprouts and serve with plain rice.

Gammon Steaks with Fresh Pineapple Sauce Rub 1 tablespoon oil over 4 cooked gammon steaks and cook under a preheated hot grill for 2–3 minutes on each side until lightly browned. Mix 250 g (8 oz) pineapple chunks with 1 tablespoon finely chopped red onion, ½ finely chopped green chilli, a large handful of chopped fresh coriander and 5 tablespoons pineapple juice and season. Spoon over the steaks to serve.

Minced Pork and Pineapple Wraps Use a mandolin to cut ½ peeled pineapple into very thin rounds. Set aside. Heat 1 tablespoon oil in a frying pan, add 300 g (10 oz) minced pork and cook over a hight heat for 7 minutes until starting to brown. Add 2 crushed garlic cloves, 1 teaspoon finely grated fresh root ginger, ½ deseeded and finely chopped red chilli and 1 finely chopped lemon grass stalk and cook for 1 minute. Pour in 2 tablespoons Thai fish sauce and 5 tablespoons pineapple juice and leave to cook until bubbled away. Stir through a handful of chopped fresh coriander. Separate the leaves of a Little Gem lettuce. Put a heaped spoonful of pork on each pineapple slice, place on a lettuce leaf with some coriander leaves, roll up and serve.

 # Roasted Sausages with Polenta

Serves 4

1 tablespoon olive oil
8 sausages
150 g (5 oz) cherry tomatoes
150 g (5 oz) fresh pepper pesto
50 ml (2 fl oz) water
1.2 litres (2 pints) vegetable stock
300 g (10 oz) instant polenta
100 ml (3½ fl oz) mascarpone
salt

- Toss together the oil and sausages in an ovenproof tin and cook in a preheated oven, 200°C (400°F), Gas Mark 6, for 12 minutes. Give the tin good shake, add the tomatoes and cook for 7 minutes more until the sausages are browned and the tomatoes are starting to wilt. Remove from the tin and keep warm.

- Add the pesto to the tin with the measurement water and stir together until warmed.

- Meanwhile, heat the stock in a large saucepan with salt to taste. Add the polenta and simmer for 5 minutes, stirring frequently, until thickened like mashed potatoes. Stir through the mascarpone.

- Spoon the polenta on to serving plates. Top with the sausages and tomatoes and drizzle over the pesto.

Chorizo and Polenta Grill

Cut 500 g (1 lb) ready-cooked polenta into thick strips. Brush with 1 tablespoon olive oil and cook on a preheated griddle pan for 2 minutes on each side until lightly charred. Keep warm. Slice 150 g (5 oz) chorizo and griddle for 1 minute on each side until browned. Toss 125 g (4 oz) halved cherry tomatoes and 150 g (5 oz) rocket leaves with 1 tablespoon balsamic vinegar and 3 tablespoons extra virgin olive oil and season to taste. Serve the salad with the chorizo and polenta.

Bacon, Polenta and Corn Cakes

Cook 4 streaky bacon rashers under a preheated hot grill for 5 minutes until just cooked through and chop into small pieces. Meanwhile, place 150 g (5 oz) each plain flour and polenta, 2 teaspoons baking powder, 2 eggs, 75 g (3 oz) melted butter and 300 ml (½ pint) buttermilk in a food processor and whizz together until smooth. Season to taste. Drain a 125 g (4 oz) can of sweetcorn and stir into the batter with the bacon. Spoon into a well-greased 12-hole muffin tray and cook in a preheated oven, 200°C (400°F), Gas Mark 6, for 20–25 minutes or until just cooked through. Serve with sliced tomatoes and a green salad.

Grilled Lamb with Minted Peas

Serves 4

2 tablespoons olive oil
1 onion, finely chopped
1 garlic clove, crushed
250 ml (8 fl oz) chicken stock
500 g (1 lb) frozen peas
handful of mint leaves, chopped
2 × 300 g (10 oz) lamb fillets
50 g (2 oz) feta cheese, crumbled
salt and pepper

- Heat 1 tablespoon oil in a saucepan, add the onion and cook for 5 minutes until softened. Stir in the garlic and cook for 1 minute more. Add the stock and simmer for 2–3 minutes, add the peas and cook for 3 minutes until soft. Reserve some of the peas, then whizz the remainder with a stick blender until nearly smooth. Stir in most of the mint and season to taste.

- Rub the remaining oil over the lamb and season well. Cook under a preheated hot grill for 5-7 minutes on each side until browned and just cooked through.

- Slice the lamb and arrange on serving plates with the pea mash. Scatter over the reserved peas, remaining mint and feta to serve.

10 Lamb with Pea Salad

Rub 2 teaspoons oil over 8 small lamb chops. Cook under a preheated hot grill for 3–5 minutes on each side until golden and charred. Meanwhile, cook 150 g (5 oz) frozen peas in lightly salted boiling water for 3 minutes until soft. Drain and cool under cold running water. Whisk together 3 tablespoons olive oil with a good squeeze of lemon juice and season to taste. Toss with 125 g (4 oz) pea shoots, a handful of chopped mint, 1 sliced spring onion and the cooled peas. Scatter over 50 g (2 oz) crumbled feta cheese and serve with the chops.

30 Spring Lamb Stew

Heat 1 tablespoon oil in a saucepan, add 1 chopped onion and cook for 5 minutes until softened. Halve 150 g (5 oz) Chantenay carrots and add to the pan with 500 g (1 lb) new potatoes. Pour over 350 ml (12 fl oz) vegetable stock. Bring to the boil and simmer for 15–20 minutes until the vegetables are soft. Add 150 g (5 oz) frozen peas and cook for a further 3 minutes until soft. Meanwhile, rub 1 tablespoon oil over 2 lamb loins. Cook under a preheated hot grill for 5 minutes on each side until golden and cooked through, then cut into thick slices. Stir some chopped parsley and mint through the stew and top with the lamb.

30 Rack of Lamb with Harissa Dressing

Serves 4–6

125 g (4 oz) hazelnuts
75 g (3 oz) sesame seeds
2 tablespoons coriander seeds
1 tablespoon cumin seeds
4 tablespoons olive oil
2 racks of lamb
2 red peppers, cored, deseeded
  and thickly sliced
2 tablespoons harissa
5 tablespoons natural yogurt
salt and pepper
couscous, to serve

- Put the nuts and spices in a small, dry frying pan and cook for 1 minute. Transfer to a mortar and crush roughly with a pestle, adding a little salt.

- Rub 2 tablespoons oil over the lamb racks, season well and press the nut mixture on to the fatty side of each rack. Transfer to a shallow roasting tin and bake in a preheated oven, 220°C (425°F), Gas Mark 7, for 10 minutes. Arrange the peppers around the lamb and cook for 10–15 minutes more for rare to medium lamb.

- Swirl the harissa over the yogurt in a bowl. Slice the lamb racks and serve with the peppers, drizzling over the harissa sauce before serving with couscous.

---

10 Harissa Lamb Wraps

Mix 1 tablespoon lemon juice and the finely grated rind of ½ lemon with 1 tablespoon harissa and 1 tablespoon olive oil. Season to taste and toss with 375 g (12 oz) lamb leg chunks. Heat a griddle pan until smoking and cook the lamb together with 1 sliced onion for 3 minutes on each side until charred and cooked through. Heat 4 large flatbreads on the griddle pan for 30 seconds, then arrange the onions and lamb on top. Place ¼ cucumber, cut into chunks, and 100 g (3½ oz) shredded lettuce on top, drizzle over some natural yogurt, then wrap and serve.

20 Easy Spiced Lamb Pilaff

Heat 1 tablespoon olive oil in a casserole, add 1 tablespoon harissa and then 325 g (11 oz) lamb leg chunks. Stir around the pan until well coated, then stir in 300 g (10 oz) basmati rice. Pour over 600 ml (1 pint) chicken stock and bring to the boil. Leave to simmer, uncovered, for 10 minutes. Stir in 150 g (5 oz) baby spinach leaves, reduce the heat to low, cover and cook for 5 more minutes until the rice is soft. Sprinkle with mint leaves and drizzle with yogurt to serve.

Lamb Steaks with Tomatoes, Feta and Hummus Mash

Serves 4

4 tablespoons olive oil

1 onion, chopped

2 garlic cloves, crushed

½ teaspoon ground cumin

2 × 400 g (13 oz) cans chickpeas, rinsed and drained

75 ml (3 fl oz) chicken stock or water

2 tablespoons lemon juice

4 lamb leg steaks

75 g (3 oz) cherry tomatoes, halved

50 g (2 oz) feta cheese, crumbled

handful of oregano, chopped

salt and pepper

- Heat 2 tablespoons oil in a saucepan, add the onion and cook for 5 minutes until softened. Stir in the garlic and cumin and cook for a few seconds. Add the chickpeas, then pour over the stock or water and leave to simmer for 2–3 minutes until warmed through. Season to taste. Use a stick blender or transfer to a food processor and whizz to make a rough purée. Squeeze over the lemon juice and keep warm.

- Rub 1 tablespoon oil over the steaks, season and cook under a preheated hot grill for 5–7 minutes on each side until golden and just cooked through.

- Pile the tomatoes, cheese and oregano on top of the steaks. Drizzle over the remaining oil and cook under the hot grill for a further 1–2 minutes until golden. Serve with the chickpea mash.

 Lamb Burgers with Tomato Feta Salsa

Rub 1 tablespoon oil over 4 ready-made lamb burgers. Cook on a preheated griddle pan for 4 minutes on each side until cooked through. Meanwhile, toss together 125 g (4 oz) halved cherry tomatoes, 2 teaspoons red wine vinegar, 3 tablespoons olive oil, 1 crushed garlic clove, 50 g (2 oz) feta cheese and a handful of oregano. Season to taste and put the burgers in buns and top with the salsa and a handful of rocket leaves.

30 Lamb, Feta and Tomato Bake

Heat 1 tablespoon olive oil in a large, ovenproof frying pan, add 1 chopped onion and cook for 5 minutes until softened. Stir in 500 g (1 lb) minced lamb and cook for another 5 minutes, breaking up any clumps. Add 2 crushed garlic cloves and 2 teaspoons tomato purée and cook for 30 seconds more. Pour over 400 g (13 oz) can cherry tomatoes and a splash of water. Add a handful of chopped oregano, season to taste and simmer for 10–15 minutes. Scatter over 75 g (3 oz) feta cheese, cook under a preheated hot grill for 1 minute and then serve.

Lamb and Pepper Traybake with Mint Salsa

Serves 4

8 lamb noisettes
2 red peppers, cored, deseeded
    and cut into wedges
5 unpeeled garlic cloves
4 tablespoons olive oil
juice and finely grated rind of
    ½ lemon
pinch of caster sugar
½ teaspoon Dijon mustard
large handful of basil leaves,
    very finely chopped
large handful of mint leaves,
    very finely chopped
salt and pepper

- Arrange the lamb, peppers and garlic on a baking sheet. Drizzle over 1 tablespoon oil, season well and bake in a preheated oven, 200°C (400°F), Gas Mark 6, for 15–20 minutes until lightly browned and just cooked through.

- Whisk together the lemon rind and juice, the sugar and mustard and the remaining oil. Season to taste and stir through the herbs. Drizzle the dressing over the lamb and peppers and serve with new potatoes.

 Lamb and Pepper Kebabs

Core, deseed and cut 1 red pepper into squares. Thread the pepper on to barbecue skewers, alternating with 400 g (13 oz) cubed lamb. Drizzle over 1 tablespoon vegetable oil, season and cook on a smoking griddle pan for 3 minutes on each side until charred and just cooked through. Scatter over the finely grated rind of 1 lemon and a handful of chopped mint leaves before serving.

Lamb Burgers with Red Pepper Tomato Relish Core, deseed and thickly slice 2 red peppers. Heat 2 tablespoons olive oil in a saucepan, add the peppers and cook for 10 minutes. Add 125 g (4 oz) halved cherry tomatoes, a pinch of dried chilli flakes and cook for a further 10 minutes. Stir in 1 teaspoon white wine vinegar and 1 teaspoon caster sugar, season to taste and cook for a further 2–3 minutes until thick and pulpy. Meanwhile, mix together 450 g (14½ oz) minced lamb, 1 crushed garlic clove, a pinch of dried chilli flakes, a handful of mint leaves and 1 egg yolk. Form the mixture into 4 burgers, brush over 2 teaspoons olive oil and season. Cook on a hot griddle pan for 5–7 minutes on each side until cooked through. Place in buns or pitta breads, top with the relish and a handful rocket leaves and serve.

30 Individual Beef Wellingtons

Serves 4

4 thick beef tenderloin steaks
5 tablespoons mushroom pâté
4 slices of prosciutto
2 × 375 g (12 oz) packs
   ready-rolled puff pastry
1 egg, beaten
oil, for greasing
4 thyme sprigs
salt and pepper

To serve

sugarsnap peas
roasted new potatoes

- Place a heaped tablespoon of pâté on each steak and then wrap in a prosciutto slice.

- Cut each pastry sheet into 2 squares and brush with a little egg. Place a steak in the centre of each, fold over the corners of the pastry and tuck together to seal.

- Place the pastry parcels, seal side down, on a lightly greased baking sheet, brush the tops with a little more egg and top with a sprig of thyme. Bake in a preheated oven, 220°C (425°F), Gas Mark 7, for 12–15 minutes until the pastry is puffed and golden. Serve with sugarsnap peas and roasted new potatoes.

---

10 Beef and Mushroom Melts

Heat 1 tablespoon oil in a frying pan and cook 1 sliced onion for 7 minutes until soft and golden. In another frying pan cook 75 g (3 oz) sliced mushrooms for 3–5 minutes until soft. Pile the onion and mushrooms on to one half of 4 split rolls. Top with 150 g (5 oz) sliced roasted beef and 100 g (3½ oz) sliced Cheddar cheese. Place under a hot grill until the cheese starts to melt, then replace the roll tops and serve.

20 Beef Steaks with Mushroom Sauce

Heat a frying pan until it is smoking and then add 1 tablespoon oil and 15 g (½ oz) butter to the pan. Add 1 sliced onion and cook for 5–7 minutes until softened. Add 150 g (5 oz) sliced mushrooms and cook for 2 more minutes more until softened. Add 1 crushed garlic clove and cook for 30 seconds. Carefully pour over 2 tablespoons brandy and leave to bubble until reduced. Add 5 tablespoons crème fraîche and cook until thickened. Keep the sauce warm. Rub 1 tablespoon oil over 4 beef steaks and season. Cook on a smoking griddle pan for 2–3 minutes on each side until browned but still pink inside. Set the beef aside to rest, then spoon the sauce over the steaks just before serving.

10 Vietnamese Beef Skewers

Serves 4

2 lemon grass stalks
1 garlic clove, crushed
1 red chilli
1 small shallot
3 teaspoons light brown sugar
4 tablespoons Thai fish sauce
500 g (1 lb) beef steak strips
1 tablespoon oil
600 g (1 lb 3½ oz) fresh rice noodles
squeeze of lime juice
¼ iceberg lettuce, shredded
2 carrots, grated
handful of mint leaves

- Put the lemon grass, garlic, chilli, shallot, half the sugar and 2 tablespoons fish sauce in a blender and whizz to form a chunky paste.

- Rub the mixture all over the beef and thread the meat on to skewers. Drizzle over the oil. Heat a large griddle pan until smoking, then cook the skewers for 1–2 minutes on each side until charred.

- Meanwhile, cook the noodles according to the pack instructions, cool under cold running water and drain. Stir together the remaining sugar and fish sauce with the lime juice. Toss through the noodles along with the lettuce, carrots and mint leaves and serve with the skewers.

---

20 Stir-Fried Rice with Beef

In a smoking griddle pan, cook 2 large beef steaks for 2–3 minutes on each side until charred but still pink in the middle, then set aside to rest. Boil 250 g (8 oz) rice for 10 minutes until soft, then drain. Heat 1 tablespoon oil in a wok, add 1 chopped shallot and cook for 2 minutes. Add 1 finely chopped garlic clove, 2 teaspoons grated fresh root ginger, 1 finely chopped lemon grass stalk and ½ chopped red chilli and cook for 1 minute. Add 1 sliced red pepper and cook for 2 minutes. Stir in the rice and 2 tablespoons Thai fish sauce. Slice the beef and add to the pan with some chopped basil to serve.

30 Braised Vietnamese Beef

Heat 2 tablespoons oil in a saucepan, add 1 sliced onion and cook for 5 minutes until softened. Add 2 crushed garlic cloves, 2 teaspoons finely grated fresh root ginger, 1 finely chopped lemon grass stalk and 1 deseeded and chopped red chilli. Stir around the pan for 1 minute. Pour over 300 ml (½ pint) beef stock, 3 tablespoons Thai fish sauce and 1 tablespoon light brown sugar. Bring to the boil and leave to simmer for 15 minutes. Rub 1 tablespoon oil over 4 beef steaks. Heat a griddle pan until smoking, season the steaks and cook for 2–3 minutes on each side until

charred but still pink in the middle. Cut the meat into thick pieces and add to the braise for 2 minutes to heat through. Serve over plain rice.

 # Grilled Rib-Eye with Blue Cheese Butter and Spring Onion Mash

Serves 4

875 g (1¾ lb) potatoes, peeled and quartered
125 g (4 oz) crème fraîche
2 spring onions, sliced
50 g (2 oz) butter, softened
1 garlic clove, crushed
200 g (7 oz) blue cheese
25 g (1 oz) toasted walnuts, finely chopped
handful of parsley, chopped
1 tablespoon olive oil
4 rib-eye steaks
salt and pepper

- Cook the potatoes in a large saucepan of lightly salted boiling water for 12–15 minutes until soft. Mash until smooth. Reserve about 4 tablespoons crème fraîche and stir the remainder into the potatoes along with the spring onions, season to taste and keep warm.

- Meanwhile, stir together the butter, garlic and blue cheese, then add the walnuts and parsley and season to taste. Place in a sheet of clingfilm and roll up to form a cylinder. Twist the ends to seal and place in the freezer for 5–10 minutes to firm up.

- Heat a griddle pan until smoking. Rub the oil over the steaks and season well. Cook for 2–3 minutes on each side for medium rare. Leave to rest for a minute or two, then place on serving plates with the mash and top with a slice of the flavoured butter.

 Beef Salad with Blue Cheese Dressing Whisk together 6 tablespoons olive oil with 2 tablespoons white wine vinegar, crumble in 50 g (2 oz) blue cheese and stir until smooth. Heat a griddle pan until smoking. Rub 1 tablespoon oil over 8 thin frying steaks and season. Cook for 1–2 minutes on each side until seared but still just pink in the middle. Toss the dressing with 200 g (7 oz) mixed salad leaves and 50 g (2 oz) croûtons, then add 125 g (4 oz) halved cherry tomatoes and 2 sliced spring onions. Serve with the steaks.

 Steak with Blue Cheese Sauce and Onion Rings Heat 25 g (1 oz) butter in a saucepan, add 1 chopped shallot and cook for 3 minutes. Stir in 1 crushed garlic clove and cook for 1 minute more. Crumble in 200 g (7 oz) blue cheese and whisk until melted, then stir in 5 tablespoons crème fraîche and a handful of chopped chives. Keep warm. Slice 3 onions into thick rings, put them in a bowl with 500 ml (17 fl oz) buttermilk and stir until well covered. Place 200 g (7 oz) flour into a bowl with some salt and a pinch of cayenne. Heat a large saucepan, one-third full with oil, until hot enough that a cube of bread dropped into the oil will sizzle and brown in 15 seconds. Working in batches, remove some onion rings from the buttermilk and dip into the flour until well coated. Shake off any excess flour and cook the onion in the hot oil for 2–3 minutes until golden. Keep warm in the oven. Cook 4 rib-eye steaks as above. Serve with the sauce drizzled over, along with the onion rings and some lightly steamed spinach.

FOO-MEAT-WYA

3⊘ Porcini Meatballs

Serves 6

25 g (1 oz) dried porcini
  mushrooms
125 ml (4 fl oz) boiling water
75 g (3 oz) fresh white
  breadcrumbs
25 ml (1 fl oz) milk
625 g (1¼ lb) minced beef
1 egg, beaten
25 g (1 oz) grated Parmesan
  cheese, plus extra to serve
1 rosemary sprig, finely chopped
1 garlic clove, crushed
2 tablespoons olive oil
500 ml (17 fl oz) ready-made
  fresh tomato sauce
600 g (1 lb 3½ oz) spaghetti
salt and pepper

- Put the mushrooms in a small pan, cover with the measurement boiling water and simmer for 2 minutes until soft. Drain, reserving the liquid.

- Meanwhile, put the breadcrumbs in a small bowl, pour over the milk and leave for 1-2 minutes until absorbed, then mix together with the beef, egg, Parmesan, rosemary and garlic. Finely chop the porcini and stir into the mixture. Season to taste. Lightly wet your hands and form the mixture into meatballs about the size of a walnut.

- Heat the oil in a large frying pan, add the meatballs and cook for 5–7 minutes, turning occasionally, until golden all over. Strain the mushroom soaking liquid, discarding any grit, and add to the pan with the tomato sauce. Leave to simmer for 15 minutes or until the meatballs are cooked through.

- Meanwhile, cook the spaghetti according to the pack instructions. Drain, reserving a little of the cooking water, and return to the pan. Add the meatballs to the pan, together with some of the cooking water to loosen if needed. Transfer to serving bowls and scatter with Parmesan shavings.

 Grilled Mushroom and Beef Salad

Toss 200 g (7 oz) mushrooms with 3 tablespoons olive oil and season to taste. Grill for 3–5 minutes until softened and lightly charred. Whisk together 6 tablespoons olive oil with 3 tablespoons lemon juice and season. Toss the dressing with 250 g (8 oz) rocket leaves. Arrange on a plate with 400 g (13 oz) sliced rare roast beef and the mushrooms. Top with Parmesan cheese shavings.

 Steak with Creamy Mushroom and Tomato Sauce Heat 2 tablespoons olive oil in a frying pan, add 200 g (7 oz) wild mushrooms and cook for 3 minutes until golden. Add 1 chopped garlic clove and cook for 30 seconds more. Add 1 teaspoon tomato purée and 100 ml (3½ fl oz) dry white wine. Leave to bubble for 2 minutes until reduced, then stir through 5 tablespoons crème fraîche followed by

150 g (5 oz) halved cherry tomatoes. Season to taste and leave to simmer for 2 minutes or until the tomatoes have softened. Meanwhile, rub 3 tablespoons oil over 6 steaks and season well. Heat a griddle pan until smoking and cook the steaks for 2–3 minutes on each side. Cook 600 g (1 lb 3½ oz) egg noodles according to the pack instructions, drain and toss through 25 g (1 oz) butter. Serve alongside the steaks with the sauce spooned over.

30 Seared Beef Fillet with Horseradish Sauce and Tomatoes

Serves 4

750 g (1½ lb) new potatoes, halved

4 tablespoons olive oil

200 g (7 oz) small plum tomatoes, halved

2 teaspoons balsamic vinegar

1 teaspoon caster sugar

750 g (1½ lb) thin beef fillet

2–3 tablespoons horseradish sauce

100 ml (3½ fl oz) crème fraîche

salt and pepper

- Toss the potatoes with 2 tablespoons oil, season and place on a baking sheet. Cook in a preheated oven, 200°C (400°F), Gas Mark 6, for 20 minutes. Put the tomatoes, cut side up, on the baking sheet, drizzle over 1 tablespoon olive oil, then sprinkle over the vinegar and sugar. Cook for a further 5 minutes until the potatoes are soft and the tomatoes are lightly charred.

- Meanwhile, heat a large, ovenproof frying pan until smoking. Season the beef well, then swirl the remaining oil around the pan and add the beef. Cook for 1 minute on each side until browned all over, then transfer the pan to the oven and cook for 12–15 minutes for medium rare. Leave the beef to rest for a couple of minutes, then cut into thick slices.

- Stir together the horseradish sauce and crème fraîche. Arrange the beef on a plate along with the tomatoes and potatoes. Serve with the horseradish sauce.

---

10 Roast Beef Salad with Horseradish Dressing Cook 125 g (4 oz) green beans in boiling water for 3–5 minutes until just soft. Drain and cool under cold running water. Toss the beans with 150 g (5 oz) rocket leaves, 2 chopped tomatoes, 3 tablespoons olive oil and 1 tablespoon lemon juice. Arrange on a platter with 200 g (7 oz) sliced roast beef. Mix 3 tablespoons horseradish sauce with 5 tablespoons soured cream, 2 tablespoons milk and a handful of chopped chives. Drizzle over the salad to serve.

20 Seared Steak with Horseradish Mash Cook 875 g (1¾ lb) peeled and quartered potatoes in a large saucepan of boiling water for 12–15 minutes until soft. Mash and stir in 125 ml (4 fl oz) crème fraîche and 1–2 tablespoons horseradish sauce. Meanwhile, heat a large frying pan until smoking. Swirl 1 tablespoon oil around the pan. Season 4 fillet steaks really well, add to the pan and cook for 2–3 minutes on each side for medium rare. Whisk 1 tablespoon balsamic vinegar with 3 tablespoons olive oil and season. Toss together with 150 g (5 oz) watercress leaves and 125 g (4 oz) halved cherry tomatoes. Serve with the steaks and mash.

FOO-MEAT-DOK

20 Beef Strips with Tomato, Paprika and Caramelized Onion

Serves 4

2 tablespoons vegetable oil
1 onion, sliced
2 garlic cloves, crushed
2 teaspoons tomato purée
1 teaspoon caster sugar
1 teaspoon smoked paprika
150 g (5 oz) cherry tomatoes
3 large rump steaks
3 tablespoons brandy
100 ml (3½ fl oz) soured cream
salt and pepper
plain boiled rice, to serve

• Heat 1 tablespoon oil in a large frying pan and cook the onion over a low heat for 15 minutes until really soft. Stir in the garlic, tomato purée, sugar and paprika and cook for a further 1 minute. Add the cherry tomatoes and cook for 2 minutes or until starting to wilt. Carefully add the brandy to the pan and cook for 1 minute until reduced down.

• Meanwhile, heat the remaining oil in another large pan, add the steaks and cook for 3 minutes on each side until golden but still pink in the middle. Set aside for a couple of minutes to rest.

• Cut the steak into thick strips and arrange on serving plates, then spoon over the tomato sauce and soured cream. Serve with plain rice.

10 Creamy Beef and Tomato Toasts

Lightly toast 4 large pieces of sourdough bread. Toss 150 g (5 oz) cherry tomatoes with 1 tablespoon olive oil and 1 crushed garlic clove in a roasting tin, season to taste and cook under a preheated hot grill for 2 minutes until the tomatoes start to burst. Arrange 150 g (5 oz) sliced roasted beef on the bread and spoon over the tomato mixture. Then spoon 1 tablespoon soured cream over each toast and top with a sprinkling of paprika and some rocket leaves to serve.

30 Creamy Tomato and Beef Pasta

Bake Heat 1 tablespoon oil in a large frying pan, then add 400 g (13 oz) minced beef and cook for 5 minutes or until browned. Add 2 finely chopped garlic cloves and 1 teaspoon each tomato purée and paprika and cook for 1 minute more. Pour over 400 g (13 oz) can chopped tomatoes and simmer for 10 minutes, then stir in 2 tablespoons crème fraîche. Meanwhile, cook 300 g (10 oz) penne according to the pack instructions. Drain and mix with 200 g (7 oz) crème fraîche and 2 tablespoons water to loosen the mixture. Spoon the beef into an ovenproof dish, top with the pasta and sprinkle over 75 g (3 oz) grated mozzarella cheese and a handful of grated Parmesan. Cook under a hot grill for 3–5 minutes until golden.

QuickCook
Fish

Recipes listed by cooking time

30

20

10

1 Seared Prawns with Squid Ink Pasta

Serves 4

400 g (13 oz) squid ink spaghetti
5 tablespoons olive oil
3 garlic cloves, finely chopped
1–2 red chillies, deseeded and
  chopped
200 g (7 oz) large raw peeled
  prawns
75 ml (3 fl oz) dry white wine
handful of parsley, finely chopped
salt

- Cook the pasta in a large pan of lightly salted boiling water according to the pack instructions.

- Meanwhile, heat the oil in a large frying pan, add the garlic and chillies and cook for 30 seconds. Add the prawns and cook for 1–2 minutes on each side until turning golden. Add the wine and cook until nearly boiled away.

- Drain the pasta, reserving a little of the cooking water. Add the prawns and juices to the pan, along with a little cooking water to loosen it if necessary. Stir through the parsley and serve.

2 Salt and Pepper Prawns with Squid

Stir 75 g (3 oz) cornflour, 2 teaspoons sea salt flakes, ½ teaspoon pepper and a pinch each of Chinese five spice powder and cayenne pepper with 50 ml (2 fl oz) ice cold water. Toss 200 g (7 oz) large raw peeled prawns with 250 g (8 oz) squid, cut into rings, in the cornflour mixture. Heat a large pan one-third full of oil until a cube of bread dropped in the oil sizzles and turns brown after 15 seconds. Cook the prawns and squid, in batches, for 1–2 minutes until golden and crisp. Drain on kitchen paper and serve with lemon wedges and a green salad.

3 Squid Ink and Prawn Paella

Heat 600 ml (1 pint) fish or chicken stock in a pan with 1 teaspoon squid ink. Heat a large saucepan, add 2 tablespoons olive oil and stir in 150 g (5 oz) sliced chorizo. Cook for 1 minute. Add 1 finely chopped onion and cook for 5 minutes more until softened, then add 2 finely chopped garlic cloves and 1 finely chopped red chilli. Cook for 30 seconds and add 300 g (10 oz) paella rice. Stir around the pan until well coated. Pour the stock into the rice pan and leave to cook, uncovered, for 10 minutes. Put 150 g (5 oz) large raw peeled prawns on top with 125 g (4 oz) halved cherry tomatoes. Cover and cook for a further 5 minutes over a low heat. Stir through 150 g (5 oz) squid rings, leave for 30 seconds, then squeeze over some lemon juice, scatter with chopped parsley and serve.

30 Sea Bream in a Salt Fennel Crust with Lemon Dressing

Serves 4

2 kg (4 lb) coarse salt
1 tablespoon fennel seeds
2 egg whites, lightly beaten
2 sea bream, scaled and gutted
1 lemon
1 lime
1 orange
½ fennel bulb, thinly sliced
4 tablespoons extra virgin olive oil
handful of chives, chopped
salt and pepper

- Mix together the salt and fennel seeds and stir through the egg whites. Spread about one-third of this mixture over the bottom of a large ovenproof dish. Place the fish on top, then cover with the remaining salt, making sure you don't have any gaps, although it's fine for the tails to be showing. Bake in a preheated oven, 200°C (400°F), Gas Mark 6, for 20 minutes.

- Meanwhile, cut the peel from the citrus fruits using a sharp knife. Divide the fruits into segments by cutting between the membranes, holding them over a bowl to catch the juice. Place in the bowl with the juice and the remaining ingredients and season.

- To serve, crack open the salt crust by giving it a sharp tap with the back of a heavy knife. Peel away the salt crust, remove the fish and serve with the dressing alongside.

 Grilled Sea Bream with Fennel Salsa Verde Rub 1 tablespoon olive oil over 4 sea bream fillets and season well. Cook on a smoking griddle pan, skin side down, for 5 minutes, then turn over and cook for a further 3 minutes until charred and just cooked through. Meanwhile, finely chop ¼ fennel bulb. Mix together with 3 tablespoons olive oil, the finely grated rind of 1 lemon and 1 tablespoon lemon juice, 2 teaspoons capers and a handful of chopped parsley. Spoon over the fish to serve.

 Sea Bream Baked on Salt Spread 1 kg (2 lb) coarse salt over a baking sheet. Thinly slice 1 fennel bulb and place on top of the salt together with some thyme sprigs. Lay 4 sea bream fillets on top, skin side up, and bake in a preheated oven, 200°C (400°F), Gas Mark 6, for 10–12 minutes until the fish just starts to flake. Carefully lift off the salt, squeeze over a little lemon juice and serve.

Grilled Swordfish with Warm Romesco Salad

Serves 4

6 tablespoons olive oil

2 red peppers, cored, deseeded and quartered

2 slices of ciabatta bread, torn into chunks

1 garlic clove, crushed

1 tablespoon sherry vinegar

½ teaspoon smoked paprika

150 g (5 oz) tomatoes, chopped

4 swordfish steaks

25 g (1 oz) blanched almonds

25 g (1 oz) blanched hazelnuts

handful of parsley, chopped

salt and pepper

- Rub 1 tablespoon oil over the peppers, season and cook under a hot grill for 5–8 minutes until charred all over. Toss the bread in another tablespoon of oil and grill for 3 minutes, turn over and cook for 2 minutes more until just crisp and golden. Set aside.

- Whisk together the garlic, vinegar, smoked paprika and 3 tablespoons olive oil to form a dressing and toss together with the warm peppers and the tomatoes. Set aside.

- Rub 1 tablespoon olive oil over the swordfish steaks, season and cook under a preheated hot grill for 5 minutes on each side until golden and just cooked through.

- Meanwhile, heat a dry frying pan and cook the nuts for 2 minutes until lightly browned, then roughly chop. Toss the pepper mixture with the bread, most of the nuts and parsley. Serve alongside the fish with some more parsley and nuts scattered over.

 Grilled Swordfish with Romesco Dip

In a small food processor whizz together 1 ready-roasted red pepper with 25 g (1 oz) toasted flaked almonds, ½ slice of white bread, 3 plum tomatoes, 1 tablespoon sherry vinegar, ½ teaspoon smoked paprika and 3 tablespoons olive oil to make a smooth sauce. Season. Rub 1 tablespoon olive oil over 4 swordfish steaks and season well. Cook on a griddle pan for 5 minutes on each side or until just cooked through. Serve with the dipping sauce and a salad.

 Swordfish and Romesco Stew

Heat 2 tablespoons olive oil in a large saucepan, add 1 finely chopped onion and cook for 5 minutes until softened. Add 1 finely chopped fennel bulb and cook for a further 5 minutes. Stir in 2 crushed garlic cloves, a pinch of chilli flakes and ½ teaspoon smoked paprika. Add 1 tablespoon sherry vinegar and 125 ml (4 fl oz) dry white wine and allow to bubble away. Add 400 g (13 oz) can cherry tomatoes and simmer for a further 10 minutes. Meanwhile, grind 25 g (1 oz) toasted flaked almonds in a small food processor. Stir into the stew along with 2 chopped ready-roasted peppers and simmer for a few minutes. Then add 4 swordfish steaks and leave to cook for 5–7 minutes until just cooked through. Scatter over a handful of chopped parsley and serve with toasted ciabatta bread.

20 Manhattan Clam Chowder

Serves 4

500 g (1 lb) clams, scrubbed
125 ml (4 fl oz) dry white wine
1 tablespoon oil
125 g (4 oz) lardons
1 large onion, chopped
1 celery stick, chopped
1 carrot, peeled and chopped
3 potatoes, peeled and chopped
400 g (13 oz) can tomatoes
1 thyme sprig
1.5 litres (2½ pints) fish stock
salt and pepper
crusty bread or crackers, to serve

- Put the clams in a large saucepan with the wine, cover and cook for 5 minutes or until the clams have opened. Discard any that do not open. Remove the clam meat from most of the shells, keeping some in their shells for decoration, and reserve the juice.

- Meanwhile, heat the oil in a large saucepan, add the lardons and cook for 2 minutes until browned. Stir in the onion, celery and carrot and cook for 5 minutes more until softened. Then add the potatoes, tomatoes, thyme, stock and the cooking liquid from the clams.

- Cook for 12–15 minutes until the potatoes are soft. Season and return the clam meat and whole clams to the pan. Heat through and serve with crusty bread or crackers.

---

10 Clam and Tomato Linguine

Heat 1 tablespoon olive oil in a large pan, add 2 crushed garlic cloves and cook for 30 seconds. Add 125 ml (4 fl oz) dry white wine and 400 g (13 oz) scrubbed clams. Cover and cook for 5 minutes until the clams have opened. Discard any that do not open. Stir in 1 tablespoon lemon juice and 150 g (5 oz) halved cherry tomatoes. Cook 500 g (1 lb) fresh linguine according to the pack instructions, drain, reserving a little cooking water, then stir in the clams with 2 tablespoons butter and some cooking water if needed. Scatter over chopped parsley and serve.

30 Clam and Spicy Tomato Pizza

Mix 2 × 150 g (5 oz) packs pizza base mix according to the pack instructions and knead for 3 minutes. Divide the dough into 4 pieces, roll out each piece into a round and place on a lightly greased baking sheet. Meanwhile, heat 1 tablespoon olive oil in a large pan, add 75 ml (3 fl oz) dry white wine and 300 g (10 oz) scrubbed clams, cover and cook for 5 minutes until the clams have opened. Discard any that do not open. Remove the meat from the shells. Stir 1 tablespoon lemon juice into 500 ml (17 fl oz) ready-made fresh tomato pasta sauce along with a pinch of dried chilli flakes. Spread this over the prepared pizza bases. Scatter over 250 g (8 oz) mozzarella cut into strips and cook in a preheated oven, 220°C (425°F), Gas Mark 7, for 12 minutes until golden and crisp. Scatter the cooked clams over the pizzas and bake for a further 30 seconds to heat through.

30 Tomato and Feta Pilaff with Prawns

Serves 4

3 tablespoons olive oil
1 onion, finely chopped
2 garlic cloves, crushed
300 g (10 oz) basmati rice
125 ml (4 fl oz) dry white wine
400 g (13 oz) can chopped
   tomatoes
500 ml (17 fl oz) fish or chicken
   stock
400 g (13 oz) large raw prawns
   with shells
4 tablespoons ouzo (optional)
handful of chopped oregano
75 g (3 oz) feta cheese
pinch of dried chilli flakes
salt and pepper

- Heat 2 tablespoons olive oil in a large saucepan, add the onion and cook for 5 minutes until softened. Stir in the garlic and cook for 30 seconds more. Add the rice and stir around the pan until well coated. Pour over the wine and leave to bubble for 2–3 minutes until reduced by half.

- Add the tomatoes and stock, season and bring to the boil. Leave to cook for 10 minutes until most of the liquid has boiled away, then turn down the heat to low, cover and leave for 5 minutes until the rice is soft.

- Meanwhile, heat the remaining oil in a large frying pan. Add the prawns and cook for 2 minutes until turning golden. Turn over and carefully pour over the ouzo, if using. Cook for 2–3 minutes more until the prawns are cooked through and the ouzo has reduced. Season to taste. Transfer the rice to plates, arrange the prawns on top and then scatter over the oregano, feta and chilli flakes to serve.

---

10 Spicy Prawn and Tomato Pasta

with Feta Add 500 g (1 lb) fresh penne pasta to a large saucepan of lightly salted boiling water and cook according to the pack instructions. Add 300 g (10 oz) large raw peeled prawns for the last 3 minutes of cooking. Drain, reserving a little cooking water, and return to the pan. Stir in 150 g (5 oz) halved cherry tomatoes, a pinch of dried chilli flakes, 3 tablespoons olive oil, 100 g (3½ oz) feta cheese and a little cooking water if needed. Scatter over a handful of parsley leaves.

20 Prawn, Tomato and Feta Stew

Heat 1 tablespoon olive oil in a saucepan, add 1 finely chopped onion and cook for 5 minutes until softened. Stir in 1 crushed garlic clove and cook for 30 seconds, then add 250 g (8 oz) chopped tomatoes and cook for 5 minutes until the tomatoes have softened. Pour over 150 ml (5 fl oz) chicken or fish stock and simmer for another 5 minutes. Then add 300 g (10 oz) large raw peeled prawns and cook for 3–5 minutes until just cooked

through. Season to taste and scatter over chopped dill and parsley together with 75 g (3 oz) feta cheese before serving with plenty of crusty bread.

30 Tomato and Feta Pilaff with Prawns

Serves 4

3 tablespoons olive oil
1 onion, finely chopped
2 garlic cloves, crushed
300 g (10 oz) basmati rice
125 ml (4 fl oz) dry white wine
400 g (13 oz) can chopped
   tomatoes
500 ml (17 fl oz) fish or chicken
   stock
400 g (13 oz) large raw prawns
   with shells
4 tablespoons ouzo (optional)
handful of chopped oregano
75 g (3 oz) feta cheese
pinch of dried chilli flakes
salt and pepper

- Heat 2 tablespoons olive oil in a large saucepan, add the onion and cook for 5 minutes until softened. Stir in the garlic and cook for 30 seconds more. Add the rice and stir around the pan until well coated. Pour over the wine and leave to bubble for 2–3 minutes until reduced by half.

- Add the tomatoes and stock, season and bring to the boil. Leave to cook for 10 minutes until most of the liquid has boiled away, then turn down the heat to low, cover and leave for 5 minutes until the rice is soft.

- Meanwhile, heat the remaining oil in a large frying pan. Add the prawns and cook for 2 minutes until turning golden. Turn over and carefully pour over the ouzo, if using. Cook for 2–3 minutes more until the prawns are cooked through and the ouzo has reduced. Season to taste. Transfer the rice to plates, arrange the prawns on top and then scatter over the oregano, feta and chilli flakes to serve.

---

10 Spicy Prawn and Tomato Pasta

with Feta Add 500 g (1 lb) fresh penne pasta to a large saucepan of lightly salted boiling water and cook according to the pack instructions. Add 300 g (10 oz) large raw peeled prawns for the last 3 minutes of cooking. Drain, reserving a little cooking water, and return to the pan. Stir in 150 g (5 oz) halved cherry tomatoes, a pinch of dried chilli flakes, 3 tablespoons olive oil, 100 g (3½ oz) feta cheese and a little cooking water if needed. Scatter over a handful of parsley leaves.

20 Prawn, Tomato and Feta Stew

Heat 1 tablespoon olive oil in a saucepan, add 1 finely chopped onion and cook for 5 minutes until softened. Stir in 1 crushed garlic clove and cook for 30 seconds, then add 250 g (8 oz) chopped tomatoes and cook for 5 minutes until the tomatoes have softened. Pour over 150 ml (5 fl oz) chicken or fish stock and simmer for another 5 minutes. Then add 300 g (10 oz) large raw peeled prawns and cook for 3–5 minutes until just cooked

through. Season to taste and scatter over chopped dill and parsley together with 75 g (3 oz) feta cheese before serving with plenty of crusty bread.

20 Tandoori Salmon with Yogurt Sauce

Serves 4

2 tablespoons tandoori paste
150 g (5 oz) natural yogurt
1 teaspoon grated fresh root
  ginger
4 salmon steaks
½ cucumber, finely chopped
finely grated rind and juice of
  ½ lime
handful of fresh mint, chopped
½ teaspoon cumin seeds
1 tablespoon vegetable oil
1 carrot, cut into matchsticks
½ red onion, sliced
¼ white cabbage, shredded
handful of fresh coriander,
  chopped
salt and pepper

- Mix together the tandoori paste with 2 tablespoons yogurt and ½ teaspoon ginger and smear all over the salmon steaks. Set aside to marinate for 5–10 minutes.

- Meanwhile, mix together the remaining yogurt with the cucumber, lime rind and mint and season. Put the cumin seeds in a dry pan and cook for 30 seconds until aromatic. Whisk together the remaining ginger with the lime juice, oil and toasted cumin seeds to make a salad dressing. In a separate bowl toss the carrot, onion, cabbage and coriander with the dressing.

- Cook the salmon under a preheated hot grill for 3–5 minutes until lightly charred. Turn over and cook for 3 minutes more until browned and cooked through. Serve with the salad and the yogurt sauce.

---

10 Salmon Salad with Yogurt Dressing

Thinly slice ½ cucumber and toss together with 150 g (5 oz) mixed salad leaves and 250 g (8 oz) flaked poached salmon. In a small bowl, stir together 5 tablespoons natural yogurt with 1 tablespoon oil, 1 finely chopped red chilli, 1 crushed garlic clove and 1 teaspoon grated ginger. Add 1 tablespoon lime juice, season and drizzle over the salad. Serve with crusty bread.

30 Salmon Kedgeree with Yogurt

Heat 1 tablespoon vegetable oil in a large saucepan and cook 1 finely chopped onion for 5 minutes until softened. Add 2 crushed garlic cloves, 1 teaspoon grated fresh root ginger and 1 teaspoon each ground coriander and cumin, a pinch of turmeric and 4 cardamom pods. Cook for 30 seconds, then add 300 g (10 oz) basmati rice. Stir around the pan until well coated. Pour over 600 ml (1 pint) fish or chicken stock, season to taste, bring to the boil and simmer for 10 minutes until most of the liquid has boiled away. Cover and leave for 5 minutes. Meanwhile, heat a pan of water until boiling. Add 8 quails' eggs and cook for 4 minutes, drain, cool under cold running water and remove the shells. Halve the eggs and stir into the rice with 200 g (7 oz) chopped smoked salmon and 25 g (1 oz) diced butter. Spoon on to serving plates, drizzle over 4 tablespoons natural yogurt and sprinkle with dried chilli flakes and chopped fresh coriander.

20 Italian Fish Stew

Serves 4

3 tablespoons olive oil

1 leek, sliced

4 garlic cloves, sliced

1 teaspoon fennel seeds

2 tablespoons sun-dried tomato
  purée

125 ml (4 fl oz) dry white wine

300 ml (½ pint) fish stock

handful of oregano, chopped

300 g (10 oz) cherry tomatoes,
  halved

300 g (10 oz) sea bream fillet

500 g (1 lb) mussels

8 large cooked prawns with shells

150 g (5 oz) squid, cut into rings

To serve

chopped parsley

crusty bread

- Heat the oil in a large saucepan, add the leek and cook for 3–5 minutes until soft. Stir in the garlic and fennel seeds and cook for 30 seconds. Stir in the tomato purée and cook for 1 minute more. Add the wine and bubble for 1–2 minutes, then pour over the stock and leave to simmer for 5 minutes.

- Add the oregano, tomatoes, sea bream and mussels. Cover and cook for 3 minutes. Add the prawns and cook for 2 minutes more. Discard any mussels that do not open. Stir in the squid and heat through. Sprinkle over the parsley before serving with plenty of crusty bread.

 Griddled Fish with Fennel and Tomato Salsa Finely chop 1 fennel bulb and mix together with 4 tablespoons extra virgin olive oil, a handful of chopped basil and 6 chopped sun-blush tomatoes. Season to taste. Rub 1 tablespoon oil over 4 thin fish fillets. Cook on a hot griddle pan for 2–3 minutes on each side until just cooked through. Spoon over the salsa and serve.

 Whole Sea Bream Baked in Tomato and Fennel Sauce Heat a large frying pan, add 3 tablespoons olive oil and 2 chopped fennel bulbs and cook for 5 minutes until softened. Add 3 sliced garlic cloves and 1 chopped red chilli and cook for 30 seconds. Pour over 125 ml (4 fl oz) dry white wine and allow to bubble for 2 minutes. Pour over 300 ml (½ pint) fish stock and bring to a simmer. Stir in 250 g (8 oz) cherry tomatoes and a handful of oregano leaves and season to taste. Place 2 scaled and gutted sea bream in a deep roasting tin, pour over the sauce, cover and cook in a preheated oven, 200°C (400°F), Gas Mark 6, for 20 minutes or until the fish is cooked through. Scatter over some more oregano leaves before serving.

30 Crab and Corn Cakes with Red Pepper Mayonnaise

Serves 4

2 red peppers
3 tablespoons olive oil
200 g (7 oz) frozen sweetcorn, defrosted
2 spring onions, chopped
1 egg, lightly beaten
50 g (2 oz) mayonnaise
400 g (13 oz) freshly picked crab meat
50 g (2 oz) dried breadcrumbs
50 g (2 oz) polenta
chipotle sauce, to taste
salt and pepper

- Rub the peppers with 1 tablespoon oil and cook under a preheated hot grill for 15 minutes, turning often, until charred all over. Put in a plastic bag and leave to cool a little, then peel away the skin and discard the seeds and cores.

- Mix together the sweetcorn, spring onions, egg and 2 tablespoons mayonnaise. Carefully stir in the crab meat and season to taste. Form the mixture into small cakes using your hands. Scatter the breadcrumbs and polenta over a plate, and dip each cake into the crumbs until well coated. Transfer to a plate and leave to firm in the freezer for 5 minutes.

- Whizz together the roasted peppers and remaining mayonnaise in a food processor until smooth and add chipotle sauce to taste. Heat the remaining oil in a large, nonstick frying pan and cook the cakes for 2–3 minutes on each side until crisp and golden. Serve with the red pepper mayonnaise.

---

10 Crab and Pepper Tostadas

Brush 4 corn tortillas with oil and cook them on a hot griddle pan for 30 seconds on each side until lightly charred and crisp. Chop 4 tomatoes and mix together with 1 chopped ready-roasted red pepper, the juice of ½ lime and a large handful of chopped fresh coriander. Season to taste. Place the tortillas on plates. Sprinkle over ¼ shredded iceberg lettuce. Divide 300 g (10 oz) freshly picked crab meat among them, top with sliced avocado and spoon over the pepper and tomato salsa to serve.

20 Spicy Crab and Corn Soup

Remove the kernels from 3 sweetcorn cobs using a sharp knife. Put the kernels and cobs in a large saucepan with 1.2 litres (2 pints) chicken stock and simmer for 10 minutes. Discard the cobs and remove a large spoonful of the kernels. Purée the mixture with a stick blender or food processor until smooth, then stir in 1 tablespoon soy sauce, 1 teaspoon grated fresh root ginger and 1 chopped chilli. Simmer the soup for 5 minutes. Return the corn kernels to the pan together with 250 g (8 oz) freshly picked crab meat,

2 chopped spring onions and a handful of chopped fresh coriander. Serve immediately.

10 Hot-Smoked Salmon and Watercress Pasta

Serves 4

500 g (1 lb) fresh linguine
100 ml (3 fl oz) dry white wine
125 ml (4 fl oz) crème fraîche
3 hot-smoked salmon fillets,
 flaked
finely grated rind of ½ lemon
75 g (3 oz) watercress
salt and pepper

- Heat a large pan of lightly salted water until boiling. Cook the linguine according to the pack instructions, then drain and return to the pan, reserving a little of the cooking water.

- Bring the white wine to the boil in a pan, stir through the crème fraîche and cook for 1–2 minutes, until reduced by half. Add the salmon to the pasta along with the crème fraîche sauce and lemon rind. Stir together, adding a little cooking water to loosen if needed and season to taste. Just before serving, toss through the watercress.

2 Baked Salmon with Watercress Sauce

Rub olive oil over 4 salmon fillets, season and place on a baking sheet. Cook in a preheated oven, 190°C (375°F), Gas Mark 5, for 12–15 minutes until just cooked through. Meanwhile, heat 1 tablespoon oil in a saucepan, add 1 chopped shallot and cook for 3 minutes until softened. Pour over 75 ml (3 fl oz) dry white wine and allow to bubble until nearly boiled away. Stir in 100 ml (3½ fl oz) crème fraîche and season. Whizz in a blender with 150 g (5 oz) watercress and until smooth. Leave to cool. Lightly whip 125 ml (4 fl oz) double cream, then stir in the watercress mixture and spoon over the fish.

3 Salmon and Watercress Cakes

Peel and chop 2 potatoes, boil in a pan of salted water for 10–12 minutes until soft, then roughly mash and leave to cool a little. Mix the potato with 450 g (14½ oz) flaked poached salmon, 1 egg yolk and 75 g (3 oz) finely chopped watercress leaves. Season to taste and use your hands to shape the mixture into 8 fishcakes. Set aside in the refrigerator for 5–10 minutes to firm up. Dust each cake with a little flour. Put 1 beaten egg in a shallow dish and 125 g (4 oz) breadcrumbs in another. Dip the cakes in the egg and then the breadcrumbs, coating all over. Heat 2 tablespoons oil in a large, nonstick frying pan, add the fishcakes and cook for 3–5 minutes until golden. Turn over and cook for 3–5 minutes more until golden and cooked through. Serve with lemon wedges.

FOO-FISH-BYM

Roasted Hake with Tomatoes and Pistou

Serves 4

4 thick hake steaks
25 g (1 oz) pitted black olives
100 ml (3½ fl oz) olive oil
125 g (4 oz) cherry tomatoes
2 garlic cloves, peeled
bunch of basil, stems discarded
salt and pepper
new potatoes, to serve

- Place the hake in a large roasting tin and scatter over the olives. Drizzle with 1 tablespoon oil, season and bake in a preheated oven, 200°C (400°F), Gas Mark 6, for 12–15 minutes until the fish is just cooked through. For the last 5 minutes of the cooking time, add the tomatoes to the roasting tin and drizzle over another tablespoon of oil.

- Meanwhile, put the garlic in a small food processor with a little salt and the basil and whizz until a paste forms. Add the remaining oil, a little at a time, and whizz to incorporate.

- Arrange the fish on plates with some boiled potatoes, and drizzle over the sauce to serve.

Grilled Hake with Olive Basil Salsa

Rub 1 tablespoon olive oil over 4 hake steaks, season and cook on a smoking griddle pan for 5 minutes on each side until just cooked through. Meanwhile, mix together 1 crushed garlic clove, 1 chopped tomato, 25 g (1 oz) chopped, pitted olives, ½ teaspoon red wine vinegar, a handful of chopped basil and 4 tablespoons olive oil. Season and spoon over the fish to serve.

Summery Hake and Tomato Stew

Heat 2 tablespoons olive oil in a large, deep frying pan, add 1 sliced onion and 1 sliced fennel bulb and cook for 7 minutes until softened. Stir in 1 teaspoon tomato purée and 1 crushed garlic clove, then add 125 ml (4 fl oz) dry white wine. Allow to boil until reduced by half. Add a 400 g (13 oz) can chopped tomatoes and a strip of orange rind. Leave to simmer for 5–10 minutes, then add 4 hake steaks, season, cover and cook for 12–15 minutes or until the fish is just cooked through. Scatter over some chopped basil and serve.

30 Smoked Haddock and Spinach Tart

Serves 4

375 g (12 oz) skinless, boneless smoked haddock
150 g (5 oz) frozen leaf spinach
125 ml (4 fl oz) crème fraîche
3 eggs, beaten
2 spring onions, sliced
375 g (12 oz) ready-rolled puff pastry
salt and pepper

- Put the haddock in a pan, cover with boiling water and simmer for 3 minutes. Remove the fish from the pan and flake. Pour boiling water over the spinach until wilted, then squeeze away all the excess water.

- Mix together the crème fraîche, beaten eggs (reserving 1 tablespoon) and spring onions and season well. Mix half this mixture with the spinach. Unwrap the pastry on to a baking sheet. Score a 1 cm (½ inch) border around the edges with a sharp knife and brush the border with the reserved egg.

- Spoon the spinach mixture into the centre of the tart and scatter the haddock on top. Spoon over the remaining crème fraîche mixture and bake in a preheated oven, 200°C (400°F), Gas Mark 6, for 20 minutes or until golden and cooked through.

 Smoked Haddock and Spinach Gnocchi

Place 300 g (10 oz) skinless, boneless smoked haddock in a pan, cover with boiling water and simmer for 5 minutes until just cooked through, then break the fish into large flakes. Heat a large pan of lightly salted boiling water and cook 500 g (1 lb) gnocchi according to the pack instructions. Add 150 g (5 oz) baby spinach leaves, drain and return to the pan. Add the haddock along with 75 ml (3 fl oz) crème fraîche and 1 teaspoon wholegrain mustard. Stir to coat and serve.

 Smoked Haddock and Spinach Gratin

Put 4 small boneless smoked haddock fillets on a lightly greased baking sheet. Heat 1 tablespoon each butter and oil in a large frying pan, add 200 g (7 oz) baby spinach and cook for 2–3 minutes until starting to wilt. Drain and mix with 125 ml (4 fl oz) crème fraîche and a couple of tablespoons of milk until smooth. Spoon over the haddock and bake in a preheated oven, 200°C (400°F), Gas Mark 6, for 12–15 minutes until the fish is just cooked through.

20 Goan Prawn and Coconut Curry

Serves 4

1 teaspoon cumin seeds
3 cardamom pods
2 onions, roughly chopped
4 tablespoons vegetable oil
1 bay leaf
6 curry leaves
2 cm (1 inch) piece of fresh root
    ginger, peeled and chopped
3 garlic cloves, peeled
½ teaspoon ground turmeric
1 red chilli, deseeded and chopped
200 ml (7 fl oz) coconut milk
125 g (4 oz) tomatoes, halved
400 g (13 oz) raw prawns, peeled
1 tablespoon butter
fresh coriander leaves, chopped
boiled rice, to serve

- Put the cumin and cardamom in a small frying pan and cook for 30 seconds until aromatic. Remove and set aside. Whizz the onions and 2 tablespoons oil in a food processor until smooth. Heat the remaining oil in a pan, add the onion paste, bay leaf and curry leaves and cook for 7–10 minutes until light brown.

- Meanwhile, whizz the ginger and garlic in a small food processor until smooth. Add to the pan with the toasted spices, turmeric, chilli, coconut milk, tomatoes and 150 ml (5 fl oz) water. Simmer for 5 minutes, then add the prawns and cook for 3 minutes until cooked through. Stir in the butter until melted. Scatter over the coriander leaves and serve with plain rice.

---

10 Seared Prawns with Coconut Salad

Mix 5 teaspoons ground cumin and a pinch of ground turmeric with 1 tablespoon oil. Rub over 400 g (13 oz) raw peeled prawns. Season, then cook on a smoking griddle for 1–2 minutes on each side until pink and cooked through. Whisk 3 tablespoons oil with 2 tablespoons lime juice and a pinch of sugar and season. Toss through 150 g (5 oz) salad leaves, ½ sliced cucumber and 1 chopped red chilli. Sprinkle over 25 g (1 oz) lightly toasted desiccated coconut and serve with the prawns.

30 Spicy Baked Prawn Cakes

Put 1 shallot in a food processor with 2 tablespoons oil and whizz to a smooth paste. Heat 1 tablespoon vegetable oil in a pan and cook the onion paste for 7 minutes until golden brown. Meanwhile, whizz 1 cm (½ inch) fresh root ginger and 2 peeled garlic cloves until smooth and stir into the pan for the last 2 minutes of cooking. Leave to cool a little. Whizz 500 g (1 lb) raw peeled prawns and 1 tablespoon desiccated coconut together with the cooled onion paste, 1 teaspoon ground cumin, a pinch of ground turmeric and a handful of fresh coriander to make a chunky mixture. Season well. Lightly grease a 12-hole muffin tray and divide the mixture between the holes. Cook in a preheated oven, 180°C (350°F), Gas Mark 4, for 12–15 minutes until golden and cooked through.

Charred Tuna with Peperonata

Serves 4

5 tablespoons olive oil

1 onion, thinly sliced

3 garlic cloves, chopped

3 red peppers, halved

½ teaspoon dried chilli flakes

400 g (13 oz) can cherry
 tomatoes

4 tuna steaks

salt and pepper

rocket salad, to serve

- Heat 4 tablespoons oil in a frying pan, add the onion, garlic and peppers and cook over a low heat for 10 minutes until soft and golden. Add the chilli flakes and tomatoes, season to taste, cover and leave to simmer for 10 minutes. Uncover and cook for 5 minutes more until very soft and most of the liquid has boiled away.

- Meanwhile, rub the remaining oil over the tuna steaks and season thoroughly. Heat a griddle pan until smoking and cook the tuna steaks for 2–3 minutes on each side until charred but still pink inside. Serve the tuna with the peperonata and a rocket salad.

 Tuna Pasta with Red Pepper Pesto

Cook 500 g (1 lb) fresh spaghetti in a large pan of lightly boiling salted water according to the pack instructions. Drain, reserving 1 tablespoon of water, and return to the pan. Whizz 50 g (2 oz) toasted flaked almonds in a food processor with 2 ready-roasted red peppers, 1 tablespoon olive oil and 4 tablespoons crème fraîche. Season to taste. Add the pesto to the pasta with the cooking water, if needed, and 200 g (7 oz) drained canned tuna. Stir through 75 g (3 oz) rocket leaves and serve.

 Spicy Tuna Pepper Stew

Thoroughly drain a 400 g (13 oz) can of tuna and mix with 1 egg yolk, 1 chopped spring onion, 1 chopped ready-roasted red pepper and a pinch of dried chilli flakes. Season well. Use your hands to form the mixture into about 12 walnut-sized balls. Heat 2 tablespoons vegetable oil in a large, nonstick frying pan, add the tuna balls and 1 chopped red pepper and cook for 5 minutes, turning often, until golden. Stir in 3 sliced garlic cloves and cook for 30 seconds. Pour over a 400 g (13 oz) can cherry tomatoes and leave to simmer for 10 minutes. Scatter over chopped basil leaves and serve with rice or crusty bread.

Thai-Style Squid Salad

Serves 4

50 g (2 oz) soft brown sugar
50 ml (2 fl oz) boiling water
1 garlic clove, crushed
2 teaspoons finely chopped fresh
  root ginger
1 red chilli, chopped
finely grated rind and juice of 1 lime
3 tablespoons Thai fish sauce
300 g (10 oz) prepared squid
1 tablespoon oil
½ red onion, thinly sliced
150 g (5 oz) cherry tomatoes,
  halved
200 g (7 oz) salad leaves
handful of fresh coriander
salt and pepper

- Stir together the sugar and water until the sugar dissolves. Put the garlic, ginger, chilli and lime rind into a bowl and pour over the syrup. Put in the refrigerator to cool, then stir through the lime juice and fish sauce.

- Meanwhile, cut the squid pouches in half. Score a criss-cross pattern across the inside of the squid with a sharp knife, taking care not to cut all the way through, then cut into bite-sized pieces. Rub the oil over the squid and season well. Cook on a smoking griddle pan for 1–2 minutes until charred and just cooked through.

- Put the onion, tomatoes, salad leaves and coriander on a plate. Arrange the squid on top and drizzle over the dressing before serving.

 ### Thai Seafood Broth with Noodles

Heat 1 tablespoon oil in a pan, add 2 tablespoons Thai red curry paste and cook for 1 minute. Pour over 750 ml (1¼ pints) fish stock and bring to the boil. Add 1 lemon grass stalk, 2 lime leaves, 1 teaspoon caster sugar and 1 tablespoon Thai fish sauce. Leave to simmer for 10 minutes. Remove the lemon grass and lime leaves. Pour over 400 ml (14 fl oz) coconut milk and heat through. Add 200 g (7 oz) raw peeled prawns and 125 g (4 oz) sugarsnap peas and cook for 2 minutes. Then add 500 g (1 lb) ready-cooked rice noodles and cook for 1 minute. Stir in 150 g (5 oz) sliced squid, cook for 30 seconds more, then ladle into bowls. Top with a handful of chopped fresh coriander and a handful of bean sprouts.

 ### Marinated Thai Squid

Slice 300 g (10 oz) squid into rings. Put in a bowl with the juice of ½ orange and 1 lime, and 2 tablespoons Thai fish sauce. Leave to marinate for 25 minutes until the squid turns opaque, then toss with 1 tablespoon finely chopped red onion, ½ sliced red chilli, a handful of chopped fresh coriander and 150 g (5 oz) halved cherry tomatoes. Mix a little of the marinating liquid with 2 tablespoons olive oil, season and toss through 150 g (5 oz) aromatic salad leaves. Add the drained squid and serve.

30 Monkfish with Saffron Risotto and Gremolata

Serves 4

3 tablespoons olive oil
1 onion, finely chopped
2 garlic cloves, finely chopped
2 teaspoons tomato purée
300 g (10 oz) risotto rice
125 ml (4 fl oz) dry white wine
pinch of saffron threads
900 ml (1½ pints) hot chicken or
  fish stock
500 g (1 lb) skinless, boneless
  monkfish tail
finely grated rind of 1 lemon
handful of parsley, chopped
salt and pepper

- Heat 2 tablespoons oil in a large pan, add the onion and cook for 5 minutes until softened. Stir in 1 chopped garlic clove and the tomato purée and cook for 30 seconds. Stir in the rice and cook for 2 minutes until the rice is well coated.

- Pour the wine into the pan and cook until it has bubbled away. Add the saffron, then gradually stir in the hot stock, a little at a time, stirring frequently and allowing the rice to absorb the stock before adding more.

- Meanwhile, heat the remaining oil in a large frying pan. Cut the monkfish into large cubes, add to the pan, season and cook for 1–2 minutes on each side until golden. Remove from the pan. Add the remaining stock to the rice along with the fish and cook for a further 5 minutes until the rice and fish are cooked through.

- Mix together the remaining chopped garlic with the lemon rind and parsley. Spoon the rice and fish on to plates and scatter over the gremolata to serve.

10 Gremolata Grilled Monkfish with Saffron Mayonnaise

Cut a 500 g (1 lb) monkfish tail into thick slices. Mix 1 crushed garlic clove, the finely grated rind of 1 lemon and a handful of parsley with 1 tablespoon olive oil. Season and smear the mixture all over the fish and cook on a smoking griddle for 3 minutes on each side. Meanwhile, pour 1 tablespoon boiling water over a pinch of saffron threads and leave for 1 minute. Crush 1 garlic clove and mix with 6 tablespoons mayonnaise. Add the saffron water and a good squeeze of lemon juice. Divide 150 g (5 oz) rocket leaves between 4 plates. Drizzle over the saffron mayonnaise, top with the grilled fish and serve with plenty of crusty bread.

20 Baked Saffron Monkfish Fillets

Pour 1 tablespoon boiling water over a pinch of saffron threads and leave for 1 minute. Mix with 6 tablespoons natural yogurt, 1 teaspoon ground cumin, a pinch of dried chilli flakes, 1 crushed garlic clove and 1 tablespoon lemon juice. Season and rub over 4 × 200 g (7 oz) monkfish fillets. Marinate for 5–10 minutes. Shake off excess marinade, drizzle with oil and cook in a preheated oven, 200°C (400°F), Gas Mark 6, for 10 minutes until cooked through.

Cod Fillets with Tomatoes and Salsa Verde

Serves 4

4 thick cod fillets
4 plum tomatoes, halved
1 tablespoon olive oil
salt and pepper

Salsa verde

2 canned anchovy fillets
1 garlic clove, peeled
1 teaspoon capers, drained
1 tablespoon Dijon mustard
1 tablespoon white wine vinegar
100 ml (3½ fl oz) extra virgin
   olive oil
large handful of parsley, finely
   chopped
large handful of basil, finely
   chopped

- Season the cod and put it in a lightly greased baking dish along with the tomatoes. Drizzle over the oil and cook in a preheated oven, 200°C (400°F), Gas Mark 6, for 15 minutes until the fish is opaque and just cooked through.

- Chop the anchovies, garlic and capers very finely to form a rough paste. Mix together with the mustard and vinegar, then stir in the oil, followed by the herbs.

- Drizzle the sauce over the fish fillets and tomatoes to serve.

Salsa Verde Cod Skewers Cube 400 g (13 oz) thick, skinless, boneless cod fillets and toss together with 3 tablespoons olive oil, the finely grated rind of 1 lemon, 1 crushed garlic clove and large handful each of chopped parsley and basil. Season well and thread on to skewers. Cook on a hot griddle for 3 minutes on each side until just cooked through. Squeeze over a little lemon juice and serve.

Baked Cod and Tomatoes with Herb Sauce Lightly oil 4 large pieces of kitchen foil. Thinly slice 1 onion and divide between the sheets. Place 4 thick cod fillets on top, then scatter over 4 sliced tomatoes, season and add a thyme sprig and a little more oil to each. Carefully fold up each piece of foil, leaving a little gap, and place on a baking sheet. Pour 2 tablespoons dry white wine into each parcel and seal, leaving a little space around the fish. Bake in a preheated oven, 200°C (400°F), Gas Mark 6, for 20 minutes until just cooked through. Meanwhile, place 1 finely chopped shallot, 1 tablespoon white wine vinegar and 25 ml (1 fl oz) dry white wine in a pan and boil until reduced to 2 tablespoons. Cut 125 g (4 oz) cold butter into cubes and whisk into the sauce, a cube at a time, until the sauce is thick and creamy. Add a handful each of chopped parsley and basil and 1 teaspoon capers. Season and spoon over the fish to serve.

Salmon, Dill and Rice Parcels

Serves 4

250 g (8 oz) ready-cooked plain rice

2 spring onions, chopped

finely grated rind of 1 lemon

handful of dill, chopped

4 thin skinless, boneless lightly smoked salmon fillets

50 g (2 oz) butter, melted

3 tablespoons olive oil

4 sheets of filo pastry

salt and pepper

peas and sugarsnap peas, to serve

- Mix together the rice, spring onions, lemon rind and dill. Cut the salmon into large chunks and stir through the rice.

- Stir together the melted butter and oil. Unwrap 1 pastry sheet, leaving the remainder covered with a damp, but not wet, piece of kitchen paper. Brush all over with the butter mixture, then sprinkle a quarter of the rice mixture along one short side. Fold in the long sides of the pastry and roll up to enclose the filling completely.

- Place on a baking sheet and brush with some more butter. Repeat with the remaining mixture and pastry. Bake in a preheated oven, 220°C (425°F), Gas Mark 7, for 15 minutes until golden and crispy. Serve with peas and sugarsnap peas.

 Salmon and Rice Salad

Prepare 250 g (8 oz) ready-cooked rice according to the pack instructions, transfer to a sieve and cool under cold running water. Cook 125 g (4 oz) broad beans in a pan of boiling water for 3 minutes until soft, drain and cool under cold running water. Stir with the rice and 150 g (5 oz) flaked hot-smoked salmon. Add 1 chopped spring onion, a handful of chopped dill, the finely grated rind of ½ lemon and 1 tablespoon lemon juice.

 Salmon Pasta Bake with Crunchy Lemon Dill Topping Cook 400 g (13 oz) penne according to the pack instructions, drain and return to the pan. Stir through 200 ml (7 fl oz) crème fraîche and 6 tablespoons water to make a smooth sauce. Add 150 g (5 oz) smoked salmon cut into strips and tip into a baking dish. Mix together 75 g (3 oz) dry breadcrumbs, the finely grated rind of 1 lemon and a handful of chopped dill. Scatter the mixture over the pasta and drizzle with

1 tablespoon melted butter. Cook in a preheated oven, 200°C (400°F), Gas Mark 6, for 15 minutes until bubbling and golden.

30 Baked Sea Bass with Tomatoes, Olives and Oregano

Serves 4

1.5 kg (3 lb) whole sea bass, scaled and gutted
2 tablespoons olive oil
2 oregano sprigs, chopped
pinch of dried chilli flakes
1 lemon, sliced
125 g (4 oz) cherry tomatoes
75 g (3 oz) pitted Kalamata olives
salt and pepper

To serve

olive-oil roasted potatoes
green salad

- Use a sharp knife to cut 3 slashes across each side of the fish. Mix together the olive oil, oregano and chilli and rub all over the fish. Season well, place in an ovenproof dish, scatter around the lemon slices and bake in a preheated oven, 220°C (425°F), Gas Mark 7, for 10 minutes.

- Add the tomatoes and olives and return to the oven for 10–15 minutes until the fish is just cooked through. Serve with new potatoes roasted in olive oil and a green salad.

 Grilled Sea Bass with Tomato and Olive Sauce Brush 1 tablespoon olive oil over 4 sea bass fillets and season well. Cook, skin side down, on a smoking griddle for 5 minutes until crisp. Turn over and cook for a further 3 minutes or until the fish is just cooked through. Meanwhile, toss together 150 g (5 oz) chopped tomatoes, 2 teaspoons red wine vinegar, 3 tablespoons olive oil, 50 g (2 oz) roughly chopped pitted olives, 1 teaspoon drained capers and a handful of chopped oregano leaves. Season and drizzle the sauce over the fish to serve.

 Mediterranean Sea Bass Stew Heat 2 tablespoons olive oil in a large casserole, add 1 finely chopped onion and cook for 5 minutes until softened. Add 1 chopped red pepper and cook for 2 minutes more. Stir in 2 crushed garlic cloves and 1 teaspoon tomato purée and cook for 30 seconds. Pour over 125 ml (4 fl oz) dry white wine and leave to bubble until reduced by half. Add a 400 g (13 oz) can cherry tomatoes and a pinch of sugar and leave to simmer for 2–3 minutes. Add 450 g (14½ oz) sea bass fillet, cut into chunks, and 50 g (2 oz) pitted olives, season and leave to cook for 2 minutes or until the fish is just cooked through. Stir through a handful of oregano leaves and serve.

Tea-Smoked Salmon

Serves 4

8 tablespoons rice
8 tablespoons muscovado sugar
6 tablespoons tea leaves
4 salmon fillets
3 tablespoons rice wine vinegar
1 teaspoon caster sugar
½ cucumber, sliced into thin
    ribbons
100 g (3½ oz) radishes, halved
handful of bean sprouts
handful of fresh coriander leaves,
    chopped
1 red chilli, chopped

- Line a large wok with 4 sheets of kitchen foil. Put the rice, muscovado sugar and tea leaves in the bottom of the wok. Turn on the extractor fan, place a tight-fitting lid on the wok and heat over a medium heat for about 5 minutes until the mixture is smoking.

- Lightly season the salmon fillets. Put an oiled rack or steamer basket in the wok with the salmon fillets inside. Put the lid back on the wok and leave to smoke for 8–10 minutes until the fish is just cooked through.

- Stir together the vinegar and caster sugar until the sugar has dissolved. Toss together with the remaining ingredients and serve alongside the salmon fillets.

Salmon Fillets Poached in Tea

Pour 1 litre (1¾ pints) boiling water over 4 green tea bags. Stir in a 1.5 cm (¾ inch) piece of fresh root ginger, peeled, and press down on the tea bags to extract the flavour. Put 4 salmon fillets in a shallow pan, pour over the tea mixture and simmer for 8 minutes until the salmon is just cooked through. Remove from the poaching liquid and serve with a cucumber salad and plain rice.

Tea-Smoked Salmon Fishcakes

Peel and chop 2 potatoes, boil in a pan of salted water for 10–12 minutes until soft, then roughly mash and leave to cool a little. Prepare the tea-smoked salmon as above, then remove the skin and tear the fish into flakes. Mix together with the potatoes, 1 egg yolk and a large handful of chopped fresh coriander leaves. Form the mixture into 8 small fishcakes, dust all over with 75 g (3 oz) plain flour and dip each cake in 1 beaten egg. Finally, coat in 125 g (4 oz) panko breadcrumbs. Heat 2 tablespoons vegetable oil in a pan and cook the fishcakes for 3 minutes on each side, until golden. Serve with wedges of lime for squeezing over.

10 Prosciutto-Wrapped Scallops with Peppers and Bean Mash

Serves 4

2–3 tablespoons olive oil
2 garlic cloves, finely chopped
2 × 400 g (13 oz) cans cannellini
   beans, rinsed and drained
100 ml (3½ fl oz) hot chicken
   stock
50 ml (2 fl oz) single cream
lemon juice, to taste
1 red pepper, cut into wedges
12 slices of prosciutto
12 large prepared scallops
salt and pepper
handful of rocket leaves, to serve

- Heat 1 tablespoon oil in a pan, add the garlic and cook for 30 seconds. Add the beans, stock and cream and cook for 3 minutes until the beans are warmed through. Use a stick blender to whizz to a creamy paste, season and add lemon juice to taste.

- Meanwhile, rub a little oil over the pepper and place on a smoking griddle. Cook for 2 minutes on each side until charred and soft. Wrap a prosciutto slice around each scallop, securing with a cocktail stick if needed. Rub over a little oil and cook on the griddle with the pepper for 2 minutes on each side until just cooked through. Serve with the beans and a few rocket leaves alongside.

2 Scallops with Salsa and Prosciutto

Rub 1 tablespoon olive oil over 2 red peppers and cook under a hot grill for 12 minutes, turning occasionally, until charred. Place in a plastic bag and leave to cool a little, then remove the skin and seeds. Chop the flesh and mix with 1 tablespoon sherry vinegar, 3 tablespoons olive oil and 1 teaspoon chopped thyme leaves. Fry 4 slices of prosciutto in 1 tablespoon olive oil for 1 minute on each side until crispy, then remove from the frying pan. Add 12 large scallops to the pan and cook for 2 minutes on each side until just cooked through. Chop the prosciutto, scatter over the scallops and serve with the salsa.

3 Red Pepper and Scallop Paella

Heat 2 tablespoons olive oil in a large, deep pan, add 125 g (4 oz) chopped chorizo and cook for 2 minutes until golden. Add 1 chopped onion and cook for 5 minutes until softened. Stir in 2 chopped garlic cloves and cook for 30 seconds more. Add 1 chopped red pepper and 300 g (10 oz) paella rice and stir around the pan. Pour over 600 ml (1 pint) chicken or fish stock and a pinch saffron threads. Stir to combine, season, then leave to simmer for 10 minutes until most of the liquid has been absorbed. Add 250 g (8 oz) clams to the pan along with 8 large raw peeled prawns.

Cook for 5 minutes until the seafood and rice is cooked through. Discard any clams that do not open. Add 12 baby scallops and stir through. Cook for 1 minute more until the scallops are cooked, scatter with chopped parsley and serve.

Sesame-Crusted Tuna with Ginger Dressing

Serves 6

800 g (1 lb 10 oz) piece of tuna
2 tablespoons vegetable oil
3 tablespoons white sesame seeds
3 tablespoons black sesame seeds
½ cucumber, sliced into ribbons
2 avocados, sliced
2 spring onions, shredded
salt and pepper

Dressing

1 garlic clove, crushed
1 chilli, deseeded and finely
  chopped
1 teaspoon finely chopped
  fresh root ginger
1 tablespoon soy sauce
juice of ½ lime
1 teaspoon grated orange rind
1 tablespoon honey
1 tablespoon sesame oil

· Season the tuna. Heat the oil in a large frying pan, add the tuna and cook for 3–5 minutes or until browned all over. Put the sesame seeds on a plate and press the seared tuna into them until well coated. Cook in a preheated oven, 220°C (425°F), Gas Mark 7, for 10–12 minutes until browned, but still pink inside.

· Mix together the ingredients for the dressing. Cut the tuna into thick slices and arrange on serving plates with the cucumber slices, avocados and spring onions. Drizzle over the dressing to serve.

---

1 **Tuna Carpaccio with Ginger Salad**

Cut 600 g (1 lb 3½ oz) fresh tuna into 1 cm (½ inch) steaks, put between 2 pieces of clingfilm and pound gently until thin. Arrange on serving plates. Whisk the juice of 1 orange and 1 lime and 1 teaspoon each finely chopped fresh root ginger, rice wine vinegar and soy sauce. Toss through 200 g (7 oz) rocket leaves and 150 g (6 oz) sliced radishes. Arrange on top of the tuna and sprinkle with toasted sesame seeds.

3 **Slow-Cooked Tuna Steaks with Sesame Ginger Noodles**

Rub 1 tablespoon olive oil over 6 large tuna steaks, place on a baking sheet and cook in a preheated oven, 110°C (225°F), Gas Mark ¼, for 20 minutes for rare. Meanwhile, cook 600 g (1 lb 3½ oz) udon noodles according to the pack instructions. Drain and cool under cold running water. Heat 3 tablespoons oil in a wok, add 4 finely chopped garlic cloves, 3 sliced spring onions and 3 teaspoons finely chopped fresh root ginger and cook for 30 seconds. Add the noodles to the pan with 150 g (6 oz) cooked edamame beans and stir together with 4 tablespoons light soy sauce, 1 teaspoon sesame oil and 3 teaspoons sesame seeds. Heat through and serve alongside the tuna steaks.

30 Citrus-Roasted Salmon

Serves 4

1 tablespoon olive oil
1 onion, sliced into rings
2 oranges, sliced
2 lemons, sliced
handful of thyme sprigs
1.5 kg (3 lb) piece of salmon,
   divided into 2 fillets
125 ml (4 fl oz) dry white wine
50 g (2 oz) butter
salt and pepper

To serve

crushed potatoes
green beans

- Brush a large baking sheet with the oil, place half the onion, orange and lemon on top and scatter over some thyme sprigs. Place a salmon fillet, skin side down, on top of the fruit, onion and thyme. Put the remaining fruit, onion and thyme on the fish and season well, then place the remaining salmon fillet on top. Tie some kitchen string around the fish to secure.

- Pour over the wine and dot the fish with the butter. Cook in a preheated oven, 220°C (425°F), Gas Mark 7, for 25 minutes or until just cooked through. Remove the fish to a serving plate.

- Tip the juices and bottom layer of fruit into a sieve set over a bowl. Press any extra juice from the fruit and serve over the salmon with some crushed potatoes and beans.

 Smoked Salmon with Chilli Citrus Dressing Arrange 300 g (10 oz) smoked salmon on plates. Cut 2 ripe avocados into cubes and scatter over the salmon with 75 g (3 oz) sliced radishes. In a small bowl, mix together the juice and finely grated rind of ½ lime with 3 tablespoons orange juice, 1 tablespoon soy sauce, 1 tablespoon caster sugar and 1 finely chopped red chilli. Spoon the dressing over the salmon to serve.

 Crispy Citrus Salmon Toss the finely grated rind of 1 lemon and ½ orange with 100 g (3½ oz) breadcrumbs. Stir in a handful of chopped basil. Rub 2 tablespoons olive oil over 4 large salmon fillets until well coated, season to taste, then press the breadcrumbs all over the top of the fish and drizzle with a little more oil. Place on a baking tray and cook in a preheated oven, 200°C (400°F), Gas Mark 6, for 12–15 minutes or until the fish is just cooked through.

20 Grilled Lobster with Herb Butter

Serves 4

100 g (3½ oz) butter, softened
1 garlic clove, crushed
1 tablespoon lemon juice
large handful of chopped parsley
large handful of chopped chives
2 cooked lobsters
salt and pepper

To serve

green salad with fennel
potato wedges

- Mix together the butter, garlic, lemon juice and herbs and season. Place in a sheet of clingfilm, roll into a cylinder and twist the ends to seal. Put in the freezer for 5 minutes to harden a little.

- Snap the claws away from the lobsters and crack the shell with the back of a heavy knife to remove the meat inside. Cut each lobster body in half lengthways. Wash out the head cavities with cold water and divide the claw meat between them.

- Put the lobsters on a grill pan, cut side up, slice the butter and place on top. Cook under a preheated hot grill for 5–7 minutes until bubbling. Serve with green salad and potato wedges.

10 Lobster, Herb and Chilli Salad

Carefully remove the meat from 2 cooked lobster tails and thickly slice. Cut 2 avocados into thick slices and arrange on a plate with a handful of mixed salad leaves and ½ cucumber cut into ribbons with a vegetable peeler. Place the lobster meat on top of the salad leaves and vegetables. Whisk 2 tablespoons emon juice with 4 tablespoons olive oil, a handful of chopped basil and ½ finely chopped red chilli. Season and drizzle over the salad to serve.

30 Lobster with Creamy Herb Sauce

Cut 2 cooked lobsters in half lengthways and remove the meat from the tails. Crack the claws, remove the meat and cut into chunks. Melt 25 g (1 oz) butter in a saucepan, add 25 g (1 oz) plain flour and cook for 2 minutes. Whisk in 300 ml (½ pint) milk and leave to simmer for 5–7 minutes until thickened. Heat 25 g (1 oz) butter in another pan, add 1 chopped shallot and cook for 3 minutes until soft. Add 1 crushed garlic clove, pour over 125 ml (4 fl oz) dry white wine and cook for 5 minutes or until reduced down. Stir this into the white sauce, add 4 tablespoons double cream, season and heat through. Take off the heat and add 2 egg yolks, the lobster meat and a handful each of chopped tarragon and parsley. Put the lobster shells on a baking sheet and divide the lobster mixture between them. Sprinkle over a little grated Parmesan cheese, then cook under a preheated hot grill for 5–7 minutes until golden and bubbling.

QuickCook
Vegetarian

Recipes listed by cooking time

30

20

10

30 Baked Tomato and Spinach Puffs

Serves 4

4 tablespoons extra virgin olive oil, plus extra for greasing

6 sun-blush tomatoes

150 g (5 oz) baby leaf spinach

400 g (13 oz) ricotta cheese

3 eggs, beaten

25 g (1 oz) Parmesan cheese, grated

50 g (2 oz) pitted black olives, chopped

1 tablespoon capers, rinsed and drained

handful of basil leaves, chopped

salt and pepper

To serve

mixed salad

toasted pine nuts

- Lightly grease 4 dariole moulds or ramekins. Place a tomato in the bottom of each and finely chop the remainder. Put the spinach in a sieve and pour over boiling water until wilted, then squeeze out any excess liquid. Beat together the ricotta and eggs, preferably with an electric hand whisk, for 1–2 minutes until light and airy.

- Finely chop the spinach and stir into the ricotta along with the chopped tomatoes and Parmesan. Season to taste. Spoon the mixture into the prepared moulds, place on a baking sheet and bake in a preheated oven, 190°C (375°F), Gas Mark 5, for 20 minutes until lightly puffed.

- Mix together the oil, olives, capers and basil and season to taste. Ease the baked puffs out of the moulds and place on serving plates. Drizzle over the sauce and serve with a mixed salad, scattered with toasted pine nuts.

---

1 Spinach and Tomato Pizza

Arrange 4 soft flour tortillas on nonstick baking sheets and spoon 300 ml (½ pint) fresh pasta sauce on top. Place 125 g (4 oz) baby spinach in a sieve and pour over boiling water until wilted. Squeeze out excess liquid and then arrange on the sauce. Scatter over 125 g (4 oz) sliced mozzarella cheese and 50 g (2 oz) ricotta cheese. Place under a preheated hot grill and cook for 5 minutes until the cheese has melted and the sauce is bubbling.

2 Roasted Tomato and Spinach Salad

Quarter 6 plum tomatoes and place on a baking sheet. Drizzle over 2 tablespoons olive oil, season and cook in a preheated oven, 200°C (400°F), Gas Mark 6, for 15 minutes until soft. Meanwhile, cook 125 g (4 oz) green beans in lightly salted boiling water for 3–5 minutes until just soft. Drain and cool under cold running water. Whisk together 1 tablespoon red wine vinegar, 3 tablespoons extra virgin olive oil and 1 teaspoon Dijon mustard. Toss the dressing

through 175 g (6 oz) baby spinach leaves and the beans. Arrange on a plate, top with the tomatoes, crumble over 50 g (2 oz) ricotta cheese and scatter over some toasted pine nuts to serve.

FOO-VEGE-POD

 # Creamy Walnut and Rocket Pasta

Serves 4

400 g (13 oz) orecchiette
125 g (4 oz) walnut pieces
1 garlic clove, crushed
4 tablespoons extra virgin olive oil
75 ml (3 fl oz) double cream
50 g (2 oz) grated Parmesan
  cheese
100 g (3½ oz) rocket leaves
salt and pepper

- Cook the orecchiette in a large saucepan of lightly salted boiling water according to the pack instructions.

- Meanwhile, place most of the walnuts, the garlic, oil, cream and grated Parmesan in a small blender and whizz until smooth. Season to taste.

- Drain the pasta, reserving a little of the cooking water, then stir through the walnut sauce, adding a little cooking water if needed. Toss in the rocket leaves and transfer to serving bowls. Top with the reserved walnuts and serve immediately.

 Pasta with Goats' Cheese and Walnut Sauce Mix 1 crushed garlic clove with 75 g (3 oz) soft goats' cheese, 75 g (3 oz) cream cheese, 25 g (1 oz) chopped walnuts and a large handful of chopped basil. Season to taste. Cook 500 g (1 lb) fresh pasta in a large pan of lightly salted boiling water according to the pack instructions. Drain, reserving a little of the cooking water. Return to the pan and stir through the sauce, adding a little cooking water if needed. Top with more basil and sprinkle over some more goats' cheese to serve.

 Gnocchi with Walnut, Chilli and Rocket Pesto Cook 625 g (1¼ lb) small, unpeeled potatoes in a large saucepan of boiling water for 15 minutes until soft. Drain well, peel and mash until smooth. Add 300 g (10 oz) plain flour, a pinch of salt and 50 g (2 oz) grated Parmesan cheese and mix to a soft dough. Divide into 4 and roll into long cylinders. Cut into small pieces, about 2 cm (¾ inch) long, and press down gently on each one with the tines of a fork to make a ridged surface. Cook the gnocchi in a large saucepan of lightly salted boiling water for about 3 minutes until they rise to the surface of the pan. Remove with a slotted spoon. Meanwhile, whizz 75 g (3 oz) toasted walnuts in a food processor with 100 g (3½ oz) rocket leaves, 1 deseeded and finely chopped chilli, 50 g (2 oz) grated Parmesan cheese, 1 crushed garlic clove and 5 tablespoons extra virgin olive oil. Season, toss the pesto through the gnocchi and serve with some more rocket leaves scattered over.

 # Courgette and Feta Fritters

Serves 4

1 egg, lightly beaten
25 g (1 oz) self-raising flour
2 tablespoons buttermilk
2 large courgettes, grated
handful of fresh dill, chopped
3 spring onions, chopped
150 g (5 oz) feta cheese
75 ml (3 fl oz) olive oil
toasted pitta breads, to serve

Pepper salad

2 ready-roasted peppers,
   chopped
1 tablespoon lemon juice
2 tablespoons olive oil
handful of mint leaves, chopped

- Mix together the egg, flour and buttermilk until smooth. Place the courgettes in a clean tea towel and squeeze to remove excess water, then mix into the batter along with the dill and spring onions. Crumble in the cheese.

- Heat half the oil in a large nonstick frying pan. Add heaped tablespoons of the mixture to the pan and press down a little on each fritter with the back of the spoon to flatten slightly. Cook for 3 minutes until golden brown, then turn and cook for 2 minutes more until golden and cooked through. Drain on kitchen paper and keep warm. Repeat with the remaining mixture and oil.

- Stir together the roasted peppers, lemon juice, oil and mint. Serve alongside the fritters with some toasted pitta breads.

 Tangy Couscous, Courgette and Feta Salad Slice 2 courgettes into long, thin strips. Rub with 2 tablespoons olive oil and cook on a hot griddle pan for 1 minute on each side until lightly charred. Place 300 g (10 oz) couscous in a bowl and pour over 400 ml (14 fl oz) hot vegetable stock. Cover and leave for 5 minutes, then stir in 4 tablespoons lemon juice, 5 tablespoons olive oil and a handful each of chopped parsley and mint. Season and add 75 g (3 oz) sun-blush tomatoes and the courgettes. Scatter over 50 g (2 oz) toasted pine nuts and 100 g (3½ oz) crumbled feta.

 Courgette Frittata with Dill, Feta and Olive Salsa Heat 3 tablespoons olive oil in a large, nonstick frying pan, add 1 finely chopped onion and cook for 5 minutes until softened. Meanwhile, grate 2 large courgettes. Place the courgettes in a clean tea towel and squeeze to remove excess water. Add to the pan and cook for a further 5 minutes until soft and any water has evaporated. Turn the heat to low and pour in 6 eggs, beaten with a little salt. Cook for 10–15 minutes or until the egg has set. Gently toss together a handful of dill with 75 g (3 oz) crumbled feta, 50 g (2 oz) pitted olives and 50 g (2 oz) rocket, then add a squeeze of lemon juice and 1 tablespoon olive oil. Cut the frittata into wedges and serve with the salsa on top.

10 Spicy Tofu and Mushroom Stir-Fry

Serves 4

2 tablespoons vegetable oil

250 g (8 oz) shiitake mushrooms, halved if large

1 leek (white only), thinly sliced

2 garlic cloves, chopped

2 teaspoons grated root ginger

3 tablespoons black bean sauce

1 teaspoon chilli sauce

pinch of ground Sichuan pepper

1 tablespoon cornflour

150 ml (5 fl oz) vegetable stock

2 tablespoons soy sauce

1 tablespoon rice wine vinegar

1 tablespoon caster sugar

325 g (11 oz) firm tofu, cubed

2 spring onions, shredded

plain boiled rice, to serve

- Heat the oil in a large wok, add the mushrooms and cook for 2 minutes. Add the leek and cook for 2 minutes more until softened. Stir in the garlic and ginger, followed by the black bean and chilli sauces and the Sichuan pepper.

- Mix together the cornflour, stock, soy sauce, vinegar and sugar and add to the wok. Carefully stir in the tofu. Leave to simmer for 2–3 minutes until the sauce has thickened. Sprinkle over the spring onions and serve with plain boiled rice.

20 Egg-Fried Tofu and Shiitake Rice

Boil 250 g (8 oz) rice according to pack instructions, then drain. Heat 2 tablespoons oil in a wok, add 150 g (5 oz) cubed firm tofu and cook for 3 minutes. Remove from the wok. Add 150 g (5 oz) shiitake mushrooms. Cook for 2 minutes, then add 2 chopped garlic cloves, 1 teaspoon grated fresh root ginger and 2 chopped spring onions. Cook for 1 minute. Crack 1 egg into the wok and stir until just cooked. Add the rice, tofu, 50 g (2 oz) defrosted frozen peas and 3 tablespoons soy sauce, stir and serve.

30 Spicy Tofu Pockets

Cut 625 g (1¼ lb) firm tofu into large slices, about 2 cm (¾ inch) thick. Use kitchen paper to dab away excess moisture, then season. Add oil to a large saucepan until it is one-third deep and heat until a piece of bread browns in 15 seconds. Cook the tofu, in batches, for about 3 minutes until golden all over. Drain on kitchen paper. Heat a griddle pan until smoking and cook the tofu for 1–2 minutes on each side until charred. Set aside. Toss 50 g (2 oz) shiitake mushrooms in 2 teaspoons oil and cook on the griddle until soft, then roughly chop. Mix the mushrooms with 1 chopped spring onion. Use a sharp knife to make a slit in the side of each piece of tofu and stuff it with the mushroom mixture. Mix together 3 tablespoons dark brown sugar, 1–2 teaspoons chilli sauce, 2 tablespoons tamarind sauce and 3 tablespoons dark soy sauce. Drizzle the sauce over the tofu pockets to serve.

Chickpea Falafel Wraps

Serves 4

1 red onion, thinly sliced
2 tablespoons lemon juice
2 × 400 g (13 oz) cans chickpeas, rinsed and drained
2 teaspoons ground cumin
3 spring onions, chopped
1 egg, beaten
5 tablespoons olive oil
75 ml (3 fl oz) natural yogurt
2 teaspoons tahini
large handful of parsley, chopped
2 tomatoes, chopped
salt and pepper
flatbreads, to serve

· Mix together the onion and lemon juice with some salt and leave to marinate. Meanwhile, place the chickpeas, cumin and spring onions in a food processor. Season, add 1–2 tablespoons of the egg and pulse until a chunky paste forms – it should just come together but not be too wet. Shape into walnut-sized balls.

· Heat half the oil in a large, nonstick frying pan and cook half the falafel for 3–5 minutes, turning once, until golden all over. Set aside on kitchen paper and cook the remainder in the remaining oil.

· Mix together the yogurt and tahini with a little water to form a thin sauce and season. Toss the marinated onion with the parsley. Arrange the falafels on the flatbreads along with the tomatoes and onion mixture. Drizzle over the yogurt sauce to serve.

 Tomato, Chilli and Chickpea Salad

Rinse and drain a 400 g (13 oz) can chickpeas. Whisk a good squeeze of lemon juice with 4 tablespoons olive oil and toss with the chickpeas, 3 chopped tomatoes and 1 chopped red chilli. Season, place in a bowl and scatter over 50 g (2 oz) crumbled feta cheese and a large handful of chopped mint.

 Provençal Chickpea Pancake

In a large bowl, mix together 250 g (8 oz) chickpea flour, a pinch of chilli powder, 400 ml (14 fl oz) water, a pinch of salt and 3 tablespoons olive oil. Leave to rest for 5 minutes. Whisk 2 egg whites until stiff peaks form, then carefully fold into the batter. Place a 23 cm (9 inch) ovenproof frying pan in a preheated oven,

230°C (450°F), Gas Mark 8, and leave to heat up for 5 minutes. Drizzle 2 tablespoons olive oil into the hot frying pan, add ½ sliced onion and swirl around. Pour in the batter and return to the oven for 15 minutes until just setting. Drizzle over 2 tablespoons oil and brown under a preheated hot grill for 1 minute. Top with roughly chopped tomatoes and serve in wedges.

30 Butternut Risotto with Chilli and Ricotta

Serves 4

50 g (2 oz) butter
1 tablespoon olive oil
1 onion, finely chopped
325 g (11 oz) butternut squash, peeled and chopped
1 red chilli, deseeded and finely chopped
250 g (8 oz) risotto rice
100 ml (3½ fl oz) dry white wine
750 ml (1¼ pint) hot vegetable stock
50 g (2 oz) Parmesan cheese, grated
3 sage leaves, finely chopped
50 g (2 oz) ricotta cheese
salt and pepper

- Heat half the butter with the oil in a large saucepan, add the onion and cook for 5 minutes until softened. Add the squash and cook for 2 minutes more. Stir most of the chilli into the pan along with the rice and cook for 2 minutes until the rice is well coated.

- Pour the wine into the pan and cook until it has bubbled away. Gradually stir in the hot stock, a little at a time, stirring frequently and allowing the rice to absorb the stock before adding more. When the rice is soft, after about 15 minutes, stir in the remaining butter and the Parmesan and season to taste. Spoon into serving bowls, sprinkle over the sage, ricotta and remaining chilli and serve.

 1 Butternut Chilli and Ricotta Gnocchi

Cook 300 g (10 oz) chopped butternut squash in a large saucepan of lightly salted boiling water for 3 minutes. Add 500 g (1 lb) fresh gnocchi and cook for 3 minutes or according to the pack instructions. Drain and toss through 2 finely chopped sage leaves, ½ teaspoon dried chilli flakes and 25 g (1 oz) butter. Season, then spoon on to serving plates and top with dollops of ricotta and some grated Parmesan.

 2 Butternut and Ricotta Galette

Cut 250 g (8 oz) butternut squash into thin slices. Boil together with 1 finely sliced leek for 3 minutes, then drain and cool under cold running water. Mix the leek with 5 tablespoons ricotta and season to taste. Unwrap a 325 g (11 oz) sheet of ready-rolled puff pastry on a lightly greased baking sheet. Score a 1 cm (½ inch) border, then spread the leek mixture in the centre. Arrange the butternut squash on top and scatter over some finely chopped red chilli. Brush the pastry border with beaten egg and cook in a preheated oven, 220°C (425°F), Gas Mark 7, for 12–15 minutes until golden and cooked through.

Crispy Aubergine Slices with Couscous

Serves 4

25 g (1 oz) plain flour
1 egg, beaten
125 g (4 oz) dry breadcrumbs
1 teaspoon sumac (optional)
finely grated rind and juice of
  1 lemon
2 aubergines, cut into thick slices
5 tablespoons vegetable oil
200 g (7 oz) couscous
250 ml (8 fl oz) hot vegetable
  stock
3 tablespoons extra virgin olive oil
¼ cucumber, chopped
1 spring onion, chopped
large handful of mint, chopped
large handful of parsley, chopped
salt and pepper

- Put the flour and egg on separate plates. Mix together the breadcrumbs, sumac (if using) and the lemon rind on another plate. Dip the aubergine in the flour and shake to remove any excess. Season well, then dip in the egg and finally in the breadcrumb mixture, making sure each slice is well coated.

- Heat half the vegetable oil in a large, nonstick frying pan. Add half the aubergines and cook for 3–5 minutes, turning once, until golden and cooked through. Keep warm and repeat with the remaining aubergine and oil.

- Meanwhile, place the couscous in a bowl and pour over the stock. Cover and leave for 5 minutes until all the liquid has been absorbed. Pour over the lemon juice and olive oil and leave to cool a little. Stir through the cucumber, spring onion and herbs and serve alongside the aubergine.

Chargrilled Aubergine Couscous Salad Put 200 g (7 oz) couscous in a bowl and pour over 250 ml (8 fl oz) hot vegetable stock. Cover and leave for 5 minutes, then fluff up with a fork. Toss with 2 chopped ready-roasted red peppers and 1 chopped ready-roasted aubergine. Add 1 tablespoon lemon juice, 2 tablespoons extra virgin olive oil, a large handful each of mint and parsley leaves and ½ finely chopped red chilli. Season, toss through a handful of rocket leaves and crumble over some goats' cheese.

Aubergine and Chickpea Tagine with Couscous Heat 2 tablespoons olive oil in a frying pan, add 1 thickly sliced aubergine and cook for 3–5 minutes, turning once, until golden. Heat 1 tablespoon olive oil in a large saucepan and cook 1 finely chopped onion for 5 minutes until softened. Add 2 crushed garlic cloves, 1 teaspoon finely grated fresh root ginger, 1 teaspoon tomato purée and 1 teaspoon ras el hanout spice mix and cook for 30 seconds. Pour over 200 ml (7 fl oz) vegetable stock and simmer for 5 minutes. Add the aubergine and cook for a further 10 minutes. Rinse and drain 400 g (13 oz) can of chickpeas and add to the saucepan with 150 g (5 oz) halved cherry tomatoes. Simmer for 2–3 minutes until the tomatoes are soft and season. Meanwhile, put 200 g (7 oz) couscous in a bowl, pour over 250 ml (8 fl oz) hot vegetable stock and leave for 5 minutes. Fluff up with a fork, then stir in 2 tablespoons olive oil, 1 tablespoon lemon juice and a handful of chopped mint. Season and serve the couscous with the stew and some natural yogurt.

30 Two Bean Chilli with Avocado Salsa

Serves 4

2 tablespoons vegetable oil

1 onion, finely chopped

2 garlic cloves, chopped

1 red pepper, cored, deseeded and chopped

1 teaspoon ground cumin

½ teaspoon dried oregano

400 g (13 oz) can chopped tomatoes

400 g (13 oz) can black beans, rinsed and drained

200 g (7 oz) can kidney beans, rinsed and drained

1 tablespoon finely chopped dark chocolate

salt and pepper

Salsa

2 avocados, diced

1 spring onion, sliced

1 green chilli, deseeded and chopped

2 tablespoons lime juice

fresh coriander, chopped

- Heat the oil in a large saucepan, add the onion and cook for 3 minutes until starting to soften. Add the garlic and pepper and cook for 3 minutes more. Stir in the cumin and oregano, then add the tomatoes, followed by the beans. Leave to simmer for 10 minutes. Stir in the chocolate until melted and season to taste.

- Toss all the salsa ingredients together. Spoon the chilli into serving bowls and top with the salsa.

 **Spicy Bean Salad**

Rinse and drain a 400 g (13 oz) can each of pinto and kidney beans. Place in a bowl with 150 g (5 oz) halved cherry tomatoes and 2 sliced avocados. Whisk together 4 tablespoons olive oil, 3 tablespoons lime juice, ½ teaspoon cumin and ½ chopped red chilli. Season, toss with the beans and vegetables and scatter over chopped fresh coriander.

 Spicy Beanburgers with Salsa

Rinse and drain 2 × 400 g (13 oz) cans of kidney beans. Whizz the beans in a food processor with 75 g (3 oz) fresh breadcrumbs, 1 teaspoon ground cumin and a pinch of chilli powder until a rough paste forms. Season well. Wet your fingers and form the mixture into 4 large burgers. Drizzle over 1 tablespoon oil and cook under a preheated hot grill for 3–5 minutes until crisp. Turn over and cook for 3 minutes more. Serve in burger buns topped with slices of avocado, a spoonful of tomato salsa and a dollop of soured cream.

 # Sweet Potato Laksa

Serves 4

1 tablespoon oil
1 tablespoon laksa or Thai red
  curry paste
500 ml (17 fl oz) vegetable stock
400 ml (14 fl oz) can coconut milk
2 lime leaves
2 tablespoons Thai fish sauce
200 g (7 oz) sweet potato,
  peeled and chopped
400 g (13 oz) ready-cooked rice
  noodles
150 g (5 oz) sugarsnap peas
75 g (3 oz) bean sprouts
handful of fresh coriander,
  chopped
handful of mint leaves, chopped

- Heat the oil in a large saucepan, add the curry paste and cook for 1 minute, then add the stock, coconut milk, lime leaves and fish sauce. Bring to the boil, reduce to a simmer and add the sweet potato. Cook for 12–15 minutes until soft.

- Add the rice noodles and sugarsnap peas and heat through. Ladle into bowls and top with the bean sprouts and herbs.

 ### Grilled Sweet Potato Salad

Thinly slice 2 sweet potatoes and toss in 2 tablespoons oil. Season and cook on a griddle pan for 2–3 minutes on each side until soft and charred. Put 25 g (1 oz) desiccated coconut in a dry frying pan and cook for 1–2 minutes until lightly browned. Toss the sweet potato with 3 tablespoons lime juice, 1 chopped red chilli and plenty of chopped mint and fresh coriander. Scatter over the coconut to serve.

 ### Coconut and Sweet Potato Rice

Heat 2 tablespoons oil in a saucepan, add 1 finely chopped onion and cook for 5 minutes until softened. Add 2 chopped sweet potatoes and cook for a further 3 minutes. Stir in 2 teaspoons finely grated fresh root ginger and 1 tablespoon Thai red curry paste. Pour in 300 g (10 oz) rice and stir around the pan, then add a 400 ml (14 fl oz) can coconut milk and 250 ml (8 fl oz) vegetable stock and season to taste. Leave to bubble for 10 minutes, then add 75 g (3 oz) sugarsnap peas to the pan, cover and turn the heat to low. Leave for 5 minutes. Sprinkle over plenty of chopped fresh coriander and serve.

30 Pepper and Artichoke Paella

Serves 4

2 tablespoons olive oil
1 onion, finely chopped
2 garlic cloves, chopped
250 g (8 oz) paella rice
1 teaspoon smoked paprika
pinch of dried chilli flakes
pinch of saffron threads
125 ml (4 fl oz) dry white wine
400 g (13 oz) can cherry
  tomatoes
300 ml (½ pint) vegetable stock
125 g (4 oz) green beans
2 ready-roasted red peppers, cut
  into strips
4 ready-grilled artichoke hearts,
  quartered
handful of parsley, chopped
salt and pepper
lemon wedges, to serve

- Heat the oil in a deep frying pan or paella dish, add the onion and cook for 5 minutes until softened. Stir in the garlic and cook for 1 minute more. Add the rice and spices and stir around the pan until well coated. Pour over the wine and cook until bubbled away.

- Add the cherry tomatoes followed by the vegetable stock. Cover and leave to simmer for 10 minutes. Cook the beans in a saucepan of boiling water for 2 minutes until starting to soften. Add to the paella along with the peppers and artichokes and cook for 5 minutes more until the rice is soft. Season to taste, scatter over the parsley and serve with lemon wedges.

 10 Artichoke Crostini with Peppers

Drain a 400 g (13 oz) can artichokes and pulse in a food processor. Add 3 tablespoons olive oil, 3 tablespoons crème fraîche and 1 tablespoon lemon juice. Season and pulse until almost smooth. Slice a ciabatta loaf and drizzle with oil. Toast under the grill for 2–3 minutes on each side, then rub with a garlic clove. Spread with the artichoke purée and top with ready-roasted peppers and rocket.

 20 Artichoke and Pepper Frittata

Heat 3 tablespoons olive oil in a medium frying pan, add 1 chopped onion and cook for 5 minutes until softened. Add 1 chopped garlic clove, 4 ready-grilled artichokes hearts, quartered, and 2 ready-roasted red peppers, cut into strips. Cook for 2 minutes. Whisk together 6 eggs with a handful of chopped parsley. Season to taste. Turn the heat to low and pour over the egg mixture. Cook for 8–10 minutes until the eggs are just set, finishing under a hot grill if needed. Cut into wedges and serve with a rocket salad.

FOO-VEGE-TYJ

1 Asparagus Carbonara

Serves 4

1 tablespoon olive oil
2 spring onions, chopped
150 g (5 oz) fine asparagus spears
pinch of chopped tarragon
500 g (1 lb) fresh linguine
1 egg, lightly beaten
50 g (2 oz) crème fraîche
50 g (2 oz) Parmesan cheese,
  grated, plus extra to serve
salt and pepper

- Heat the oil in a large frying pan. Add the spring onions and asparagus and cook for 2–3 minutes until just cooked through. Stir in the tarragon.

- Cook the linguine in a large saucepan of lightly salted boiling water according to the pack instructions. Drain, reserving a little cooking water, and return to the pan. Add the cooked asparagus and onion, then add the egg, crème fraîche and Parmesan, season and stir together until creamy, adding a little of the pasta cooking water if needed. Spoon into bowls and scatter over more Parmesan to serve.

2 Poached Eggs with Asparagus

Toss 150 g (5 oz) asparagus spears in 2 tablespoons olive oil. Cook on a hot griddle pan for 5 minutes, turning frequently, until charred and cooked through. Whisk together 2 tablespoons lemon juice and 4 tablespoons olive oil, add 1 crushed garlic clove and season. Cut ½ baguette into small chunks, toss with 5 tablespoons olive oil and bake in a preheated oven, 200°C (400°F), Gas Mark 6, for 7–10 minutes until golden, then leave to cool. Poach 4 eggs for 4 minutes for a soft yolk, then pat dry with kitchen paper. Toss the lemon dressing with 150 g (5 oz) spinach salad and the asparagus. Arrange on plates with the eggs, croûtons and shavings of Parmesan cheese.

3 Asparagus Tarts

Cook 150 g (5 oz) asparagus tips in a small saucepan of lightly salted boiling water for 3 minutes or until soft. Drain and cool under cold running water. Meanwhile, melt 50 g (2 oz) butter in a small pan and stir in 4 tablespoons olive oil. Lightly grease 4 × 12 cm (5 inch) loose-bottomed tart tins. Brush 1 sheet of filo pastry with the butter mixture. Cut the pastry into 4 squares and arrange these in one of the tart tins. Repeat with the remaining tins. In a small bowl, mix together 5 eggs, 100 g (3½ oz) crème fraîche, a handful of mint leaves and the finely grated rind of ½ lemon and season well. Spoon the mixture into the tart cases, add the asparagus and cook in a preheated oven, 200°C (400°F), Gas Mark 6, for 15 minutes or until the pastry is crisp and the filling is just cooked through.

Miso Aubergine with Cucumber Rice Noodles

Serves 4

12 baby aubergines, halved
4 tablespoons white miso paste
3 tablespoons rice wine vinegar
2 tablespoons caster sugar
1 tablespoon sake or water
1 tablespoon sesame seeds
125 g (4 oz) soy beans
300 g (10 oz) ready-cooked rice
  noodles
½ cucumber, thinly sliced
2 spring onions, thinly sliced
salt

- Make a criss-cross pattern on the cut sides of the aubergines and place them, cut side down, on a grill pan. Cook for 7–10 minutes under a preheated hot grill until charred. Mix together the miso paste, 2 tablespoons vinegar, the sugar and sake or water. Turn the aubergines over and brush with the miso mixture. Return to the grill for 3–5 minutes until the aubergine is soft, then sprinkle with the sesame seeds and cook for 1 minute more.

- Meanwhile, cook the soy beans in a saucepan of lightly salted boiling water for 2 minutes until soft. Drain and cool under cold running water. Toss the beans together with the noodles, cucumber, spring onions, the remaining vinegar and season with salt. Serve with the grilled aubergine.

 Grilled Aubergine Salad with Miso Ginger Dressing Cut 2 large aubergines into thin slices and toss together with 6 tablespoons vegetable oil. Cook on a hot griddle pan for 2–3 minutes on each side until charred and soft. Mix together 1 tablespoon white miso paste with 2 tablespoons rice wine vinegar, a pinch of sugar, 2 teaspoons grated fresh root ginger and ½ finely chopped red chilli. Whisk in 5 tablespoons vegetable oil, then toss together with the grilled aubergine and 200 g (7 oz) rocket leaves.

 Braised Aubergine and Miso Cut 2 large aubergines into thick chunks. Heat 2 tablespoons vegetable oil in a large saucepan and cook half the aubergine pieces until lightly browned. Remove and repeat with the remaining aubergine. Add a little more oil to the pan if needed and cook 1 sliced onion for 5 minutes until softened. Stir in 2 crushed garlic cloves and 2 teaspoons finely grated fresh root ginger. Cook for 1 minute. Add 250 ml (8 fl oz) vegetable stock and leave to simmer for 10 minutes. Add 3 tablespoons white miso paste and 1–2 tablespoons caster sugar. Return the aubergine to the pan and simmer for 5 minutes until soft. Cut 2 spring onions into thin shreds and scatter over the aubergine before serving with steamed white rice.

30 Leek and Blue Cheese Tart

Serves 4

150 g (5 oz) baby leeks, trimmed
325 g (11 oz) ready-rolled puff
  pastry
oil, for greasing
1 egg, beaten
75 g (3 oz) mascarpone cheese
125 g (4 oz) blue cheese
salt and pepper

- Cook the leeks in a pan of lightly salted boiling water for 1 minute until just soft. Drain and cool under cold running water.

- Unwrap the pastry on to a lightly greased baking sheet. Use a sharp knife to lightly score a 1 cm (½ inch) border all around the pastry, taking care not to cut all the way through. Lightly mark the inside of the pastry with the end of a fork and brush all over the border with egg.

- Mix together the remaining egg, the mascarpone and half the blue cheese and spread the mixture over the pastry. Arrange the leeks on top and scatter over the remaining cheese. Cook in a preheated oven, 200°C (400°F), Gas Mark 6, for 20 minutes until the pastry is golden and cooked through.

 Creamy Leek and Blue Cheese Pasta

Cut 2 large leeks into thin slices. Cook in a large pan of lightly salted boiling water for 3–5 minutes until soft, together with 500 g (1 lb) fresh penne, cooked according to the pack instructions. Drain, reserving a little of the cooking water. Return to the pan and stir in 5 tablespoons crème fraîche, adding a little of the cooking water if needed, and crumble over 100 g (3½ oz) blue cheese. Sprinkle over some chopped parsley before serving.

 Blue Cheese, Cauliflower and Leek Bake Melt 25 g (1 oz) butter in a saucepan, add 25 g (1 oz) plain flour and stir together for 1–2 minutes, then slowly whisk in 300 ml (½ pint) milk. Cook over a low heat, stirring frequently, until the mixture thickens enough to coat the back of a spoon. Take off the heat and add 150 g (5 oz) blue cheese and stir until melted. Meanwhile, cut 1 cauliflower into florets and 2 leeks into thick chunks and cook in a saucepan of lightly salted boiling water for 5–7 minutes until cooked through. Drain and stir together with the sauce and season to taste. Tip the mixture into an ovenproof dish and scatter over 100 g (3½ oz) dried breadcrumbs and a handful of chopped thyme. Place under a medium grill, drizzle with a little oil and cook for 5 minutes until golden and bubbling.

Puffed Goats' Cheese and Red Pepper Omelettes

Serves 4

6 eggs
25 g (1 oz) grated Parmesan
  cheese
handful of basil, chopped
1 tablespoon olive oil
3 ready-roasted red peppers,
  sliced
125 g (4 oz) soft goats' cheese
salt and pepper

- Crack 3 eggs into a bowl. Separate the remaining 3 eggs and add the yolks to the whole eggs. Stir in the Parmesan and some of the basil and season to taste. Whisk the egg whites until soft peaks form, then carefully fold into the whole egg mixture, one-third at a time.

- Heat the oil in an ovenproof frying pan. Add the egg mixture and cook for 2 minutes, then scatter over the peppers and goats' cheese.

- Place the pan under a preheated hot grill and cook for 5–7 minutes more until puffed and just set. Scatter over the remaining basil to serve.

 Pecorino and Chilli Omelettes Heat 1 tablespoon butter in a small frying pan. Pour in 1 lightly beaten egg and stir around the pan. Leave to cook for 30 seconds until starting to set, then grate over 25 g (1 oz) Pecorino cheese and add a pinch of dried red chilli flakes. Cook until the omelette is set, then it roll up and keep warm. Make 3 more omelettes in the same way. Serve with a green salad.

 Red Pepper, Goats' Cheese and Spinach Bake Heat a large frying pan, add 2 tablespoons olive oil and 1 finely chopped onion and cook for 5 minutes until softened. Stir in 150 g (5 oz) baby spinach leaves and cook for 1–2 minutes until wilted. Remove the mixture from the pan and squeeze away excess water from the spinach. Beat together 150 g (5 oz) ricotta with 6 eggs, then add the spinach mixture, 25 g (1 oz) Parmesan and 2 sliced ready-roasted red peppers. Season and pour the mixture into a lightly greased ovenproof dish and crumble over 75 g (3 oz) goats' cheese. Bake in a preheated oven, 220°C (425°F), Gas Mark 7, for 10–15 minutes until set, finishing under a hot grill if needed.

Chargrilled Haloumi with Roasted Olives and Salad

Serves 4

3 garlic cloves
6 tablespoons olive oil
pinch of dried chilli flakes
finely grated rind and juice of
 ½ orange
1 teaspoon fennel seeds
100 g (3½ oz) pitted black olives
300 g (10 oz) salad potatoes,
 halved
150 g (5 oz) green beans
250 g (8 oz) haloumi cheese,
 thickly sliced
1 tablespoon red wine vinegar
125 g (4 oz) cherry tomatoes,
 halved
½ red onion, chopped
handful of oregano leaves,
 chopped
salt and pepper

- Slice 2 of the garlic cloves and mix together with 2 tablespoons olive oil, the chilli, orange rind and juice, fennel seeds and olives. Place on a small baking sheet and cook in a preheated oven, 200°C (400°F), Gas Mark 6, for 15 minutes.

- Meanwhile, cook the potatoes in a large saucepan of boiling water for 10 minutes, then add the beans and cook for 3–5 minutes more until soft. Drain and cool under cold running water. Heat a griddle pan until smoking. Pat the haloumi dry and griddle for 2–3 minutes on each side until golden and lightly charred.

- Crush the remaining garlic and whisk together with the vinegar and the remaining olive oil. Toss the dressing together with the potatoes and beans, tomatoes and onion. Arrange on a plate with the haloumi slices, drizzle over the warm olives and marinade, then scatter over the oregano to serve.

 **Fried Haloumi Sandwich**

Cut 250 g (8 oz) haloumi into thick slices. Heat 1 tablespoon olive oil in a nonstick frying pan and cook the cheese for 2–3 minutes on each side until golden. Add 1 tablespoon capers and remove from the heat. Split 4 individual baguettes. Chop 1 Little Gem lettuce and 75 g (3 oz) cherry tomatoes and place on top. Scatter over 50 g (2 oz) pitted black olives, pour over 2 tablespoons lemon juice and top with the haloumi and capers.

 Haloumi-Topped Stuffed Peppers

Core, deseed and halve 2 red peppers. Halve 4 plum tomatoes and put them with the peppers on a lightly greased baking sheet. Mix together 2 teaspoons red wine vinegar, a pinch of sugar and 1 tablespoon olive oil, drizzle over the peppers and tomatoes and cook in a preheated oven, 190°C (375°F), Gas Mark 5, for 10 minutes. Add 125 g (4 oz) pitted olives, the finely grated rind of 1 orange, a pinch of dried chilli flakes and some chopped oregano leaves. Season, drizzle over 2 tablespoons olive oil and cook for a further 15 minutes. Roughly chop the tomatoes and olives and toss through 2 teaspoons capers and a large handful each of chopped mint and dill. Fill the pepper halves with the tomato mixture. Cut 250 g (8 oz) haloumi into thin slices, top the peppers with the cheese and cook under a hot grill until browned. Serve with chopped Little Gem lettuces.

30 Puttanesca Pizza

Serves 4

2 × 150 g (5 oz) packs pizza base mix

1 tablespoon olive oil, plus extra for greasing

200 ml (7 fl oz) ready-made fresh tomato sauce

150 g (5 oz) cherry tomatoes, halved

1 red chilli, deseeded and sliced

125 g (4 oz) mozzarella cheese, sliced

50 g (2 oz) pitted olives

1 tablespoon capers

handful of rocket leaves, to serve

- Mix the pizza base according to the pack instructions and knead for 3 minutes. Roll out the dough into an oval shape, about 25 cm (10 inches) long and place on a lightly greased baking sheet. Spread over the tomato sauce and leave to rise for 5–10 minutes. Arrange the halved tomatoes, chilli, mozzarella, olives and capers on top. Drizzle over the oil.

- Bake in a preheated oven, 220°C (425°F), Gas Mark 7, for 15 minutes until the pizza is crisp. Top with the rocket leaves before serving.

---

1 **Pasta Puttanesca** Cook 500 g (1 lb) fresh penne pasta in a large saucepan of lightly salted boiling water according to the pack instructions. Drain and toss through 3 chopped tomatoes, 1 tablespoon capers, 50 g (2 oz) pitted olives, 1 tablespoon lemon juice, 4 tablespoons olive oil and a handful of chopped parsley. Season and serve immediately.

2 **Frying Pan Pizza with Puttanesca Topping** Mix 2 × 150 g (5 oz) packs pizza base mix according to the pack instructions and knead for 3 minutes. Divide into 2 balls and roll each into a round about 23 cm (9 inches) across. Heat 1 tablespoon olive oil in a large frying pan, add a pizza base and cook for 5 minutes until golden. Turn over and cook for a further 3 minutes until cooked through. Repeat with the remaining base. Spread 200 ml (7 fl oz) ready-made fresh tomato sauce over each pizza and top with 150 g (5 oz) sliced mozzarella. Cook under a hot grill for 1–2 minutes until melted, then scatter over 2 tablespoons drained capers, 50 g (2 oz) pitted olives and a handful of rocket to serve.

10 Carrot and Beetroot Tabbouleh

Serves 4

150 g (5 oz) bulgar wheat
1 garlic clove, crushed
pinch of ground cinnamon
pinch of allspice
2 tablespoons pomegranate
  molasses
5 tablespoons extra virgin olive oil
1 carrot, grated
125 g (4 oz) cooked beetroot,
  cubed
2 spring onions, sliced
½ green chilli, chopped
large handful of mint, chopped
large handful of parsley, chopped
50 g (2 oz) feta cheese
salt and pepper

- Prepare the bulgar wheat according to the pack instructions, then drain thoroughly.

- Mix together the garlic, spices, pomegranate molasses and olive oil. Toss together with the bulgar wheat, carrot, beetroot, spring onions, chilli, mint and parsley and season to taste. Scatter over the feta to serve.

---

2 Spicy Carrot Stew with Couscous

Cook 1 sliced onion, 1 sliced parsnip and 2 sliced carrots in 1 tablespoon oil for 7 minutes until soft. Stir in 2 teaspoons ras el hanout spice mix and 2 crushed garlic cloves. Pour over 300 ml (½ pint) vegetable stock and simmer for 10 minutes. Add 200 g (7 oz) cooked chickpeas and a little lemon juice and heat through. Meanwhile, pour 350 ml (12 fl oz) hot stock over 300 g (10 oz) couscous, cover and leave for 5 minutes. Stir through 25 g (1 oz) toasted flaked almonds, 1 sliced spring onion and a handful each of chopped mint and parsley.

3 Warm Roasted Carrot and Beetroot Tabbouleh

Put 150 g (5 oz) halved Chantenay carrots on a large piece of kitchen foil. Drizzle over 2 tablespoons olive oil, then fold the foil to loosely enclose. Place on a baking sheet and cook in a preheated oven, 200°C (400°F), Gas Mark 6, for 20–25 minutes until soft. Wrap 2 ready-roasted beetroot, cut into thick slices, in some foil and cook for the last 5 minutes of cooking time to heat through. Heat 2 tablespoons olive oil in a saucepan, add 1 sliced onion and cook for 10 minutes until golden and soft. Add 200 g (7 oz) bulgar wheat and pour over 250 ml (8 fl oz) boiling vegetable stock. Cover and leave to simmer for 5–10 minutes until soft. Use a fork to fluff through, then stir in 1 tablespoon lemon juice and 2 more tablespoons olive oil. Toss through the roasted vegetables and 100 g (3½ oz) rocket leaves, season to taste and scatter over 50 g (2 oz) goats' cheese to serve.

30 Roasted Cauliflower with Tomato Sauce

Serves 4

1 cauliflower, separated into florets

3 tablespoons oil

1 teaspoon cumin seeds

1 lemon, cut into wedges

1 onion, finely chopped

1 tablespoon rogan josh curry paste

400 g (13 oz) can cherry tomatoes

25 g (1 oz) cashew nuts

handful of fresh coriander, chopped

salt and pepper

boiled rice, to serve

- Put the cauliflower in a roasting tray and toss together with 2 tablespoons oil, the cumin seeds and lemon. Bake in a preheated oven, 220°C (425°F), Gas Mark 7, for 20–25 minutes until soft and lightly charred.

- Meanwhile, heat the remaining oil in a pan, add the onion and cook for 5 minutes until softened. Stir in the curry paste and cook for 1 minute. Pour over the tomatoes and leave to simmer for 15 minutes. Season to taste.

- Heat a dry frying pan and cook the cashew nuts until golden, then set aside to cool. Squeeze a couple of lemon wedges over the roasted cauliflower and pile on a plate. Spoon over the tomato sauce, scatter with the cashew nuts and fresh coriander and serve with plain boiled rice.

---

1 Spicy Cauliflower and Tomato Cheese

Separate a cauliflower into florets and cook in a large saucepan of lightly salted boiling water for 7 minutes until soft. Drain, reserving 4 tablespoons cooking water. Stir the water with 150 ml (5 fl oz) crème fraîche and 1 teaspoon garam masala and toss with the cauliflower. Place in an ovenproof dish. Arrange 1 sliced tomato on top, then cook under a hot preheated grill for 1–2 minutes until lightly browned and bubbling.

2 Cauliflower and Tomato Curry

Heat 1 tablespoon oil in a large saucepan, add 1 finely chopped onion and cook for 5 minutes until softened. Stir in 2 finely chopped garlic cloves and 2 teaspoons grated fresh root ginger. Add 1 teaspoon each ground cumin and ground coriander, ½ teaspoon ground turmeric and a pinch of cayenne pepper. Pour over 400 g (13 oz) can chopped tomatoes and season to taste. Break 1 cauliflower into florets and add to the pan. Leave to simmer for 12–15 minutes until the cauliflower is soft. Drizzle over a little natural yogurt and chopped fresh coriander and serve with some warm naan bread.

Aubergine Caponata with Ricotta

Serves 4

6 tablespoons olive oil

1 onion, sliced

2 celery sticks, sliced

1 garlic clove, sliced

2 teaspoons tomato purée

400 g (13 oz) can cherry
   tomatoes

2 aubergines, cubed

2 tablespoons white wine vinegar

2 teaspoons caster sugar

1 tablespoon capers, rinsed

125 g (4 oz) large green olives

125 g (4 oz) ricotta cheese

25 g (1 oz) toasted pine nuts

handful of basil, chopped

salt and pepper

- Heat 1 tablespoon olive oil in a large saucepan, add the onion and celery and cook for 5 minutes until softened. Add the garlic and tomato purée and cook for 1 minute more. Tip in the tomatoes, top up with a little water and leave to simmer for 5 minutes.

- Meanwhile, heat half the remaining oil in a frying pan, add half the aubergine and cook for 5 minutes, turning occasionally, until browned. Remove from the pan with a slotted spoon and leave to drain on kitchen paper. Repeat with the remaining oil and aubergine.

- Stir the vinegar and sugar into the tomato sauce, and add the cooked aubergine, capers and olives. Season to taste and leave to simmer for 7–10 minutes. Spoon into serving bowls, dollop over the ricotta and pine nuts and sprinkle with basil before serving.

Grilled Aubergine Salad with Honey and Vinegar Cut 2 aubergines into thin slices and toss with 6 tablespoons olive oil. Season well and cook on a hot griddle pan for 2 minutes on each side until soft and charred. Drizzle over 1 teaspoon clear honey, 1 tablespoon sherry vinegar and 3 tablespoons extra virgin olive oil. Scatter over 1 sliced ready-roasted red pepper, 1 deseeded and chopped chilli and a handful of chopped mint leaves. Serve with a mixed tomato and rocket salad.

Roasted Aubergine and Peppers with Tahini Dressing Slice 1 large aubergine, 1 large courgette, 2 red peppers and 1 onion and toss together with 4 tablespoons olive oil, 1 tablespoon balsamic vinegar, 2 teaspoons soft brown sugar and 2 teaspoons harissa until well coated. Place the vegetable mixture on a baking sheet, season and roast in a preheated oven, 220°C (425°F), Gas Mark 7, for 25 minutes, turning occasionally, until charred and soft. Stir through 2 tablespoons raisins. Meanwhile, mix 5 tablespoons natural yogurt with 3 tablespoons tahini, 1 crushed garlic clove and 1 tablespoon lemon juice. Stir in a handful of chopped fresh coriander and drizzle the dressing over the vegetables before serving.

10 Spicy Grilled Courgettes with Hummus Mash

Serves 4

2 × 400 g (13 oz) cans chickpeas,
  rinsed and drained
1 garlic clove, crushed
1 teaspoon ground cumin
1 tablespoon tahini
3 tablespoons lemon juice
8 tablespoons olive oil
8 baby courgettes, halved
finely grated rind of ½ lemon
1 tablespoon harissa
2 teaspoons tomato purée
handful of mint leaves
salt and pepper
lightly toasted pitta bread,
  to serve

- Warm the chickpeas in a large pan of boiling water for 1 minute and drain, reserving a little of the water. Return to the pan, reserving a few whole chickpeas. Add 75 ml (3 fl oz) of the cooking water (more if needed), the garlic, cumin, tahini, 2 tablespoons lemon juice and 4 tablespoons olive oil and whizz with a stick blender or in a food processor until a chunky purée forms. Season to taste and keep warm.

- Meanwhile, toss the courgettes with 1 tablespoon oil, season well and cook on a griddle for 2–3 minutes on each side until soft and lightly charred. Mix together the remaining oil and lemon juice, the lemon rind, harissa and the tomato purée. Arrange the chickpea mash and courgettes on plates and sprinkle the reserved chickpeas over the mash. Drizzle over the dressing and scatter with mint leaves before serving with pitta bread.

20 Vegetable and Chickpea Tagine

Cook 1 chopped onion in 2 tablespoons oil for 5 minutes until softened. Stir in 1 crushed garlic clove, 2 teaspoons ground cumin, 1 teaspoon grated fresh root ginger and a pinch of ground cinnamon. Add 400 g (13 oz) can chopped tomatoes and simmer for 5 minutes. Meanwhile, in batches, fry 1 sliced courgette, 1 aubergine, cut into chunks, and 1 red pepper, cut into chunks, until soft and lightly charred. Stir into the sauce with a 200 g (7 oz) can rinsed and drained chickpeas. Simmer for 5–10 minutes. Drizzle with natural yogurt and scatter with fresh coriander to serve.

30 Chickpea Pilaff with Courgette

Curls Heat 3 tablespoons olive oil in a large saucepan, add 1 finely chopped onion and cook for 5 minutes until softened. Stir in 2 crushed garlic cloves and cook for 30 seconds. Add 250 g (8 oz) basmati rice and stir around the pan, then pour over 750 ml (1¼ pints) vegetable stock. Bring to the boil and leave to simmer for about 10 minutes until most of the liquid has bubbled away. Add a 400 g (13 oz) can rinsed and drained chickpeas. Turn the heat to very low, cover with a lid and leave to steam for 5 minutes until the rice is soft. Meanwhile, use a vegetable peeler to slice off thin curls from 2 large courgettes. Just before serving, toss with 2 tablespoons extra virgin olive oil, 1 tablespoon lemon juice and season well. Pile the rice on to plates and top with the courgette curls. Scatter over 75 g (3 oz) crumbled feta cheese before serving.

FOO-VEGE-MAB

30 Mushroom Risotto with Gremolata

Serves 4

1 tablespoon olive oil

50 g (2 oz) butter

250 g (8 oz) wild mushrooms, halved if large

1 onion, finely chopped

300 g (10 oz) risotto rice

100 ml (3½ fl oz) dry white wine

900 ml (1½ pints) hot vegetable stock

25 g (1 oz) Parmesan cheese, grated

2 garlic cloves, finely chopped

finely grated rind of 1 lemon

large handful of parsley, chopped

salt and pepper

- Heat the oil and half the butter in a large, deep frying pan, add the mushrooms and cook for 2–3 minutes until lightly browned. Set aside. Add the onion to the pan and cook for 5 minutes until softened, then stir in the rice and cook for 2 minutes until the rice is well coated.

- Pour the wine into the pan and cook until it has bubbled away. Gradually stir in the hot stock, a little at a time, stirring frequently and allowing the rice to absorb the stock before adding more. When the rice is soft, after about 15 minutes, stir in the remaining butter, the mushrooms and the Parmesan.

- Meanwhile, mix together the garlic, grated lemon rind and parsley. Spoon the risotto into serving bowls and scatter over the gremolata.

10 Warm Mushroom and Spicy Gremolata Salad

Put 12 medium-sized field mushrooms on a lightly greased baking sheet. Mix the finely grated rind of 1 lemon, 2 tablespoons lemon juice, 1 crushed garlic clove, a handful of chopped parsley and ½ finely chopped chilli with 6 tablespoons olive oil. Drizzle over the mushrooms and season to taste. Cook in a preheated oven, 220°C (425°F), Gas Mark 7, for 8 minutes until lightly charred. Toss 200 g (7 oz) mixed salad leaves with 2 tablespoons lemon juice and some olive oil. Serve with the mushrooms and some ready-roasted red peppers.

20 Creamy Mushroom Soup with Gremolata Drizzle

Heat 25 g (1 oz) butter in a large saucepan, add 300 g (10 oz) mushrooms and cook for 2–3 minutes until lightly browned. Remove from the pan. Add 1 finely chopped onion and cook for 2 minutes, then stir in 25 g (1 oz) dried porcini mushrooms. Pour over 1.2 litres (2 pints) vegetable stock, add a sprig of rosemary and leave to simmer for 10 minutes. Return half the mushrooms to the pan along with 75 ml (3 fl oz) double cream and season to taste. Whizz with a stick blender until smooth, then add the remaining mushrooms. Mix together 3 tablespoons olive oil, 1 crushed garlic clove, the finely grated rind of 1 lemon and a handful each of chopped parsley and basil leaves. Swirl over the soup before serving.

Aubergine, Tomato and Mozzarella Melts

Serves 4

5 tablespoons olive oil
12 baby aubergines, halved
125 ml (4 fl oz) passata
75 g (3 oz) tomatoes, chopped
pinch of dried chilli flakes
handful of oregano leaves,
   chopped
200 g (7 oz) mozzarella, sliced
salt and pepper

- Rub the oil over the aubergines and season well. Place them under a hot grill and cook for 5–7 minutes on each side or until soft and golden brown.

- Mix together the passata, tomatoes, chilli and oregano and season well. Arrange the aubergines, cut side up, in the grill pan, spoon a little of the passata mixture on top of each aubergine and place some mozzarella slices on top. Return to the grill and cook for 2–3 minutes until the mozzarella has just melted.

 Aubergine Baguette Melts

Arrange 8 thick slices of ready-roasted aubergine in a grill pan. Roughly chop 2 large tomatoes and scatter them on top together with 125 g (4 oz) torn mozzarella. Cook under a hot grill for 2 minutes until the cheese melts. Lightly toast 4 individual baguettes. Place the aubergines inside together with a large handful of rocket leaves.

 Aubergine, Mozzarella and Pesto Gratin Slice 4 large aubergines into 1 cm (½ inch) strips. Heat 2 tablespoons olive oil in a large frying pan and cook the strips in batches, adding more oil if needed, for 2–3 minutes on each side until golden and soft. Arrange half the aubergines in a medium-sized gratin dish. Spoon over 125 ml (4 fl oz) passata mixed together with a pinch of dried chilli flakes, followed by 75 g (3 oz) mozzarella cut into slices. Drizzle with 4 tablespoons fresh green pesto. Top with another layer of aubergine, then another 125 ml (4 fl oz) passata. Arrange 125 g (4 oz) mozzarella on top and scatter over 50 g (2 oz) grated Parmesan. Cook in a preheated oven, 200°C (400°F), Gas Mark 6, for 15–20 minutes until golden and bubbling.

30 Broccoli, Blue Cheese and Walnut Pie

Serves 4

400 g (13 oz) broccoli florets
150 g (5 oz) watercress
150 g (5 oz) mascarpone cheese
2 eggs plus 1 egg yolk, lightly beaten
150 g (5 oz) blue cheese
25 g (1 oz) butter, melted
4 tablespoons olive oil
5 large sheets filo pastry
25 g (1 oz) walnuts, roughly chopped
salt and pepper

- Cook the broccoli in a large saucepan of boiling salted water for 2 minutes until just soft. Drain and cool under cold running water. Place the watercress in a sieve and pour over boiling water until wilted, then squeeze away excess water.

- Mix together the mascarpone and eggs and season with salt and pepper. Add the broccoli, watercress and crumble in the blue cheese. Mix together the butter and oil and brush around a 20 cm (8 inch) springform cake tin. Brush over a sheet of filo pastry, keeping the remainder of the pastry covered with a damp, but not wet, piece of kitchen paper. Put the pastry in the cake tin, letting the excess hang over the sides. Turn the tin and place another sheet, brushed with the butter mixture, on top. Repeat until the tin is lined and the pastry used up.

- Spoon the filling into the tin and pull the overhanging pastry over to cover, scrunching the corners up a little as you go. Brush over with more of the butter mixture, then scatter over the walnuts. Bake in a preheated oven, 200°C (400°F), Gas Mark 6, for 20–25 minutes until golden and crispy.

 Broccoli Blue Cheese Gratin
Boil 450 g (14½ oz) broccoli florets for 4 minutes or until soft and drain. Mix together 250 g (8 oz) crème fraîche, 125 g (4 oz) blue cheese and 3 tablespoons milk, stir through the broccoli and heat through. Place in an ovenproof dish and scatter over 50 g (2 oz) dried breadcrumbs and 25 g (1 oz) chopped walnuts, then drizzle with 1 tablespoon oil. Cook under a hot grill for 2 minutes until golden and crisp.

 Broccoli Soup with Melting Blue Cheese Bites Heat 1 tablespoon oil in a large saucepan, add 1 finely chopped onion and cook for 5 minutes until softened. Add 450 g (14½ oz) broccoli and pour over 1.2 litres (2 pints) vegetable stock. Leave to simmer for 7–10 minutes until the broccoli is really soft. Stir in 3 tablespoons crème fraîche, season to taste and use a stick blender to whizz to a smooth purée. Meanwhile, slice 1 small baguette. Under a hot grill, toast the baguette slices on one side for 1 minute until golden and crisp, then turn over and grill for 1 minute more. Mix together 150 g (5 oz) blue cheese and 4 tablespoons crème fraîche. Spread over the baguette slices and scatter over a handful of chopped walnuts. Return to the grill for 2 minutes until bubbling and melted and serve alongside the soup.

FOO-VEGE-CAK

Polenta Wedges with Onion Marmalade and Goats' Cheese

Serves 4

1 litre (1¾ pints) hot vegetable stock
250 g (8 oz) quick-cook polenta
3 tablespoons olive oil
handful of rocket leaves
150 g (5 oz) soft goats' cheese
25 g (1 oz) walnuts, toasted
6 tablespoons onion marmalade
salt and pepper

- Put the stock in a large saucepan, add the polenta and stir vigorously. Cook for 5 minutes until thickened and season to taste. Line a 23 cm (9 inch) springform cake tin with a circle of baking paper and grease the sides. Pour in the polenta. Place in the freezer for 10 minutes until cold and solid.

- Remove the polenta from the tin and cut into wedges. Brush over the wedges with 2 tablespoons olive oil, place under a preheated hot grill and cook for 2–3 minutes on each side until golden.

- Transfer to serving plates and scatter with the rocket leaves and walnuts. Crumble over the goats' cheese, drizzle over the remaining olive oil and spoon some marmalade on to each plate.

---

1 Goats' Cheese and Onion Marmalade Crostini Cut ½ ciabatta loaf into slices. Drizzle with olive oil and then toast under a hot grill for 2–3 minutes on each side until golden. Spread each slice with 1 heaped teaspoon onion marmalade and top with a slice of goats' cheese. Pop under a hot grill for 1 minute until melting, then scatter over some chopped chives to serve.

3 Polenta Wedges with Caramelized Onions Prepare the polenta wedges as above. Meanwhile, heat 1 tablespoon oil in a large frying pan set over a low heat, add 2 sliced red onions and cook for 20 minutes until browned and caramelized. Add 125 g (4 oz) light brown sugar, 125 ml (4 fl oz) red wine vinegar and 2–3 tablespoons balsamic vinegar. Increase the heat and cook for 7–10 minutes until all the liquid has been absorbed. Serve the polenta with the onions on the side.

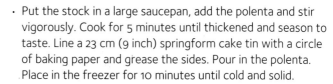

QuickCook
Puddings

Recipes listed by cooking time

30

20

10

30 Strawberry Meringue Roulade

Serves 6

4 egg whites
200 g (7 oz) caster sugar
1 teaspoon vanilla extract
300 ml (½ pint) double cream
50 g (2 oz) icing sugar, plus extra
  for dusting
3 tablespoons strawberry jam
125 g (4 oz) strawberries, sliced

- Line a 30 × 20 cm (12 × 8 inch) Swiss roll tin with baking paper. Whip the egg whites until stiff peaks appear, then add the sugar, a tablespoon at a time, and keep whisking until you have a stiff, glossy meringue. Stir through the vanilla extract.

- Spoon the mixture into the tin and smooth over the surface. Place in a preheated oven, 200°C (400°F), Gas Mark 6, and immediately reduce the temperature to 160°C (325°F), Gas Mark 3. Cook for 15 minutes until firm to the touch.

- Turn the meringue out on to a sheet of baking paper dusted with icing sugar and leave to cool for 3 minutes. Peel off the lining paper from the top of the meringue, then carefully roll up the meringue from the long side. Set aside to cool.

- Whip the double cream with the icing sugar, unroll the meringue and spread the cream on top. Mix the jam with a splash of boiling water to loosen, then spoon over the cream and top with the sliced strawberries. Using the baking paper, roll up the meringue and place on a serving plate. Dust with some more icing sugar and serve.

1 Eton Mess

Whip 600 ml (1 pint) double cream until soft peaks form. Stir in 1 teaspoon vanilla extract and 3–4 tablespoons icing sugar. Crush 4 ready-made meringue nests and place them in the bottom of 6 serving glasses. Slice 200 g (7 oz) strawberries and stir through the cream. Spoon over the meringue and top with some more sliced strawberries.

2 Strawberry Meringue Tarts

Spread 1 heaped tablespoon strawberry jam in each of 6 individual tart cases. Whip 3 egg whites until stiff peaks form. Then, a tablespoon at a time, whip in 150 g (5 oz) caster sugar until glossy and thick. Swirl the mixture over the jam. Cook in a preheated oven, 200°C (400°F), Gas Mark 6, for 5–7 minutes until the meringue is golden.

Molten Chocolate Cakes

Serves 4

125 g (4 oz) butter, plus extra
  for greasing
125 g (4 oz) plain dark chocolate,
  chopped
2 eggs
2 egg yolks
4 tablespoons sugar
2 teaspoons flour, plus extra
  for dusting
icing sugar, for dusting

- Butter and lightly flour 4 oven-proof teacups or dariole moulds. Put the butter and chocolate in a bowl set over a pan of simmering water, taking care that the bottom of the bowl does not touch the water, until the chocolate melts. Leave to cool a little.

- Use a hand-held electric whisk to beat the eggs, egg yolks and sugar until light and thick. Pour the melted chocolate mixture into the eggs, then quickly stir in with the flour until just combined.

- Spoon the batter into the moulds and bake in a preheated oven, 230°C (450°F), Gas Mark 8, for 6–7 minutes; the sides should be just set but the centres still soft. Leave to rest for a moment, then serve in the teacups, dusted with icing sugar, or invert each cake on to a plate, lift away the moulds and dust with icing sugar.

10 Chocolate Soufflé Wraps

Whisk 4 egg whites until stiff peaks form. Stir in 4 lightly beaten egg yolks, 1 teaspoon vanilla extract and 75 g (3 oz) grated plain dark chocolate. Heat 1 tablespoon butter in a small nonstick frying pan, add one-quarter of the mixture and cook for 1 minute until nearly set. Spread some ready-made chocolate sauce on the omelette and fold up. Repeat with the remaining mixture to make 4 wraps and serve with summer berries.

30 Chocolate Soufflés

Melt 175 g (6 oz) plain dark chocolate in bowl set over a pan of simmering water. Leave to cool. Grease 4 individual ramekins with a little butter, then swirl 1 tablespoon sugar around each to coat. Beat 4 egg whites until stiff, then carefully whisk in 4 tablespoons sugar until stiff and glossy. Stir 4 egg yolks into the cooled chocolate. Stir one-third of the whites into the chocolate, then gently fold in the remaining whites, half at a time, until just combined. Spoon the mixture into the moulds and run the tip of your finger around the inside edge of each mould. Bake in a preheated oven, 200°C (400°F), Gas Mark 6, for 10–12 minutes until puffed.

30 Vanilla Baked Apricots with Ricotta Cream

Serves 4

10 apricots, halved and pitted
200 ml (7 fl oz) white wine
1 teaspoon vanilla extract
125 g (4 oz) caster sugar
250 g (8 oz) ricotta
3 tablespoons double cream
2 tablespoons icing sugar

- Arrange the apricots, cut side up, in a single layer in an ovenproof dish. Heat the wine in a small saucepan. Add the vanilla extract and sugar to the pan and stir together until the sugar dissolves. Pour over the apricots and bake in a preheated oven, 190°C (375°F), Gas Mark 5, for 15 minutes or until the apricots are soft and a little browned. Leave to cool slightly.

- Put the ricotta, cream and icing sugar in a food processor and pulse until smooth. Spoon the apricots into bowls with the juices and top with the ricotta mixture to serve.

---

1 Apricot Ricotta Pots

Whizz 250 g (8 oz) ricotta and 150 ml (¼ pint) fresh custard in a food processor until smooth. Crush 125 g (4 oz) amaretti or shortbread biscuits. Sprinkle into serving bowls, reserving a few crumbs. Drizzle over 2 tablespoons Amaretto liqueur or 1 tablespoon orange juice and add 4 pitted and chopped apricots. Spoon over the ricotta mixture and top with the biscuit crumbs.

2 Ricotta Hot Cakes with Apricots

Place 200 g (7 oz) plain flour in a bowl with 1 teaspoon baking powder. Stir in 1 egg, then slowly whisk in 200 ml (7 fl oz) milk and 1 teaspoon vanilla extract until combined. Stir in 200 g (7 oz) ricotta; don't worry if there are still some lumps of ricotta. Heat a large nonstick frying pan, add 1 teaspoon oil and 1 tablespoon butter and melt. Add spoonfuls of the ricotta mixture and cook for 2–3 minutes on each side until golden and just cooked through. Remove from pan and keep warm. Repeat with the remaining mixture. Pile up on to plates and spoon over ready-made apricot compote to serve.

Coffee Cocktail with Almond Biscuits

Serves 4

175 g (6 oz) ground almonds
200 g (7 oz) caster sugar
½ teaspoon baking powder
1 egg white, lightly beaten
icing sugar, for dusting

For the cocktail

125 ml (4 fl oz) strong coffee,
  cooled
4 tablespoons coffee liqueur
4–6 tablespoons double cream

- Line a baking sheet with baking paper. Put the almonds, sugar and baking powder in a bowl and stir through the beaten egg white to make a soft paste. Knead briefly, then roll into a long cylinder. Slice off 1 cm (½ inch) pieces and lightly pinch each end to make oval shapes. Place on the baking sheet and bake in a preheated oven, 200°C (400°F), Gas Mark 6, for 10 minutes or until pale golden. Leave to cool and dust with plenty of icing sugar.

- Meanwhile, make the cocktail. Mix together the coffee and coffee liqueur and pour into 4 martini glasses. Slowly pour in the cream over the back of a teaspoon so it settles on the top. Serve with the biscuits.

 Creamy Irish Coffee

Place 1 tablespoon whiskey and 1 tablespoon caster sugar into each of 4 serving glasses. Pour over hot strong coffee and stir together. Lightly whisk 100 ml (3½ fl oz) double cream with 3 tablespoons Irish cream liqueur. Spoon over the coffee and serve with some chocolate-coated almonds.

 Chocolate Coffee Cream

Bring 300 ml (½ pint) double cream to the boil in a small pan. Pour in 3 tablespoons Kahlua, then add 100 g (3½ oz) chopped plain dark chocolate and stir until smooth. Divide between 4 serving bowls and place in the freezer for 20 minutes or until set. Whip 125 ml (4 fl oz) double cream with 1 tablespoon icing sugar, spoon over the top. Serve with almond cantuccini biscuits.

Iced Berries with White Chocolate Sauce

Serves 4

175 ml (6 fl oz) double cream
175 g (6 oz) white chocolate, chopped
½ teaspoon vanilla extract
500 g (1 lb) mixed frozen berries

- Put the cream in a small pan and heat until boiling. Take off the heat and stir in the chocolate and vanilla extract and mix until melted.

- Arrange the berries in chilled serving bowls, drizzle over the sauce and serve.

White Chocolate Berry Mousses

Melt 175 g (6 oz) white chocolate in a bowl over a pan of simmering water and leave to cool a little. Beat 200 g (7 oz) cream cheese and mix in 250 ml (8 fl oz) double cream until smooth. Stir in the cooled chocolate. In a separate bowl whisk 3 eggs with 125 g (4 oz) caster sugar until light and fluffy. Fold into the cream cheese mixture, one-third at a time. Place a handful of mixed berries in 4 serving dishes, spoon over some of the cream mixture, followed by some more berries. Keep layering and finish with shavings of white chocolate.

White Chocolate and Berry Cookies

Melt 75 g (3 oz) white chocolate in a bowl over a pan of simmering water. Leave to cool a little. Beat 100 g (3½ oz) each butter and caster sugar until fluffy, then beat in 1 egg and 1 teaspoon vanilla extract. Add 1 teaspoon baking powder and 175 g (6 oz) plain flour and stir together. Add 125 g (4 oz) chopped white chocolate and 100 g (3½ oz) dried mixed berries. Roll into small, walnut-sized balls and place on a baking sheet lined with baking paper. Bake in a preheated oven, 180°C (350°F), Gas Mark 4, for 12–15 minutes until golden. Leave to cool for 1 minute, then serve.

30 Warm Almond Cakes with Fig Compote

Serves 6

175 g (6 oz) icing sugar, sifted
75 g (3 oz) ground almonds
50 g (2 oz) plain flour
4 egg whites
125 g (4 oz) butter, melted,
   plus extra for greasing
25 g (1 oz) flaked almonds
8 figs, quartered
8 tablespoons port
1 tablespoon soft brown sugar
strip of orange rind
crème fraîche, to serve

- Grease and flour a 12-hole mini-muffin or madeleine tin. Place the icing sugar, ground almonds and flour in a mixing bowl. Stir in the egg whites until well combined, then beat in the melted butter until smooth. Spoon the batter into the tin and sprinkle a few flaked almonds on top of each cake. Bake in a preheated oven, 200°C (400°F), Gas Mark 6, for 12–15 minutes until golden.

- To make the compote put the figs, port and sugar in a small saucepan with the orange rind and cook for 5–10 minutes until soft and syrupy. Leave to cool a little. Spoon some of the compote over the cakes and serve with a spoonful of crème fraîche.

 10 Fig and Almond Trifles

Slice 125 g (4 oz) Madeira cake into small cubes and place in the bottom of 4 serving bowls. Sprinkle over 2 tablespoons orange juice and 2 tablespoons port. Roughly chop 8 figs and place on top. Whip 150 ml (5 fl oz) double cream with 1 tablespoon icing sugar until soft peaks form. Spoon 200 ml (7 fl oz) fresh custard into the bowls. Top with the cream and sprinkle with 25 g (1 oz) toasted flaked almonds before serving.

 20 Baked Figs with Almond Biscuits

Halve 8 figs and place in an ovenproof dish. Dot with 25 g (1 oz) butter and sprinkle over 2 tablespoons soft brown sugar. Pour over 4 tablespoons orange juice and 3 tablespoons port, then bake in a preheated oven, 200°C (400°F), Gas Mark 6, for 15 minutes until soft. Spoon over vanilla ice cream and serve with crisp almond biscuits.

Summer Berry Charlotte

Serves 4

625 g (1¼ lb) mixed summer
  berries
1 tablespoon flour
125 g (4 oz) caster sugar
1 teaspoon vanilla extract
4–6 slices of brioche bread
soft butter, for spreading
vanilla ice cream, to serve

· Toss together the berries, flour, sugar and vanilla extract
and place in an ovenproof dish.

· Cut the brioche slices into triangles, removing the crusts if
you like. Butter both sides of the brioche and arrange on top
of the berries. Cover the dish with foil and then bake in a
preheated oven, 220°C (425°F), Gas Mark 7, for 10 minutes.
Uncover and cook for a further 5 minutes until golden and
crisp. Serve with vanilla ice cream.

 **Berry Brioche
Toasts**

Heat 25 g (1 oz) butter in a frying
pan until melted, add 250 g
(8 oz) fresh strawberries and
blueberries and 4 tablespoons
caster sugar. Swirl around the
pan until the sugar melts and the
berries start to burst. Lightly
toast 4 thick slices of brioche
bread. Place on serving plates,
spoon over the berries with all
the juices and serve with scoops
of ice cream.

 **Simple Summer
Pudding**

Stir together 4 tablespoons
blackcurrant cordial, 300 g
(10 oz) berry compote and
500 g (1 lb) mixed berries. Leave
for a couple of minutes, then
drain, reserving the juices in a
shallow bowl. Line a 1.2 litre
(2 pint) pudding basin with
clingfilm. Cut out a circle from
a slice of brioche to fit in the
bottom of the bowl. Soak the
brioche in the fruit juices, then

place in the bowl. Cut another
6–8 slices of brioche into long
strips, dip into the juices and
use to line the sides of the basin,
then spoon in the fruit to fill.
Cover with some more brioche
slices and pour over the
remaining juice. Cover with
clingfilm, place a small plate
on top and weigh down with a
heavy can. Leave in the fridge
for 10–15 minutes, then turn
out on to a serving plate. Serve
with cream.

3 0 Sticky Toffee Cakes

Serves 4

75 g (3 oz) pitted dates
125 ml (4 fl oz) water
1 teaspoon baking soda
50 g (2 oz) butter, softened, plus extra for greasing
75 g (3 oz) light brown sugar
1 egg
1 tablespoon golden syrup
½ teaspoon vanilla extract
100 g (3½ oz) plain flour

For the sauce

50 g (2 oz) dark brown sugar
50 g (2 oz) butter
75 ml (3 fl oz) double cream

- Grease 4 individual bundt tins or pudding moulds. Put the dates and water in a small saucepan, bring to the boil and simmer for 3 minutes. Remove from the heat and add the baking soda (which will froth up). Place in the freezer to cool a little.

- Whizz together the remaining ingredients in a food processor. Add the cool dates with the cooking liquid and process until smooth.

- Spoon the mixture into the tins and cook in a preheated oven, 190°C (375°F), Gas Mark 5, for 20–25 minutes until just cooked through.

- Meanwhile, make the sauce by placing all the ingredients in a small saucepan over a low heat. Stir together until smooth and the butter has melted, then keep warm. Turn the puddings out from their moulds, spoon over some sauce and serve the rest in a jug.

 Sticky Toffee Sundaes

Heat 10 chopped pitted dates, 50 g (2 oz) dark brown sugar, 50 g (2 oz) butter and 75 ml (3 fl oz) double cream in a pan until the butter has melted. Scoop balls of vanilla ice cream into bowls, spoon over the hot sauce and top with some chopped toasted pecans.

 Roasted Sticky Dates with

Rice Pudding Heat 24 pitted dates, 200 ml (7 fl oz) dry sherry, 25 g (1 oz) soft brown sugar, 1 cinnamon stick and a piece of orange rind in a pan until boiling. Pour into a small ovenproof dish and cook in a preheated oven, 180°C (350°F), Gas Mark 4, for 15 minutes,

basting the dates a couple of times. Discard the cinnamon stick and orange rind. Stir 400 g (13 oz) can rice pudding together with 150 ml (5 fl oz) lightly whipped double cream and place in serving dishes. Spoon over the dates and sauce before serving.

20 Summer Berry Charlotte

Serves 4

625 g (1¼ lb) mixed summer
  berries
1 tablespoon flour
125 g (4 oz) caster sugar
1 teaspoon vanilla extract
4–6 slices of brioche bread
soft butter, for spreading
vanilla ice cream, to serve

- Toss together the berries, flour, sugar and vanilla extract and place in an ovenproof dish.

- Cut the brioche slices into triangles, removing the crusts if you like. Butter both sides of the brioche and arrange on top of the berries. Cover the dish with foil and then bake in a preheated oven, 220°C (425°F), Gas Mark 7, for 10 minutes. Uncover and cook for a further 5 minutes until golden and crisp. Serve with vanilla ice cream.

 Berry Brioche Toasts

Heat 25 g (1 oz) butter in a frying pan until melted, add 250 g (8 oz) fresh strawberries and blueberries and 4 tablespoons caster sugar. Swirl around the pan until the sugar melts and the berries start to burst. Lightly toast 4 thick slices of brioche bread. Place on serving plates, spoon over the berries with all the juices and serve with scoops of ice cream.

 Simple Summer Pudding

Stir together 4 tablespoons blackcurrant cordial, 300 g (10 oz) berry compote and 500 g (1 lb) mixed berries. Leave for a couple of minutes, then drain, reserving the juices in a shallow bowl. Line a 1.2 litre (2 pint) pudding basin with clingfilm. Cut out a circle from a slice of brioche to fit in the bottom of the bowl. Soak the brioche in the fruit juices, then place in the bowl. Cut another 6–8 slices of brioche into long strips, dip into the juices and use to line the sides of the basin, then spoon in the fruit to fill. Cover with some more brioche slices and pour over the remaining juice. Cover with clingfilm, place a small plate on top and weigh down with a heavy can. Leave in the fridge for 10–15 minutes, then turn out on to a serving plate. Serve with cream.

30 Chocolate Peanut Butter Whoopie Pies

Serves 6–8

300 g (10 oz) self-raising flour
50 g (2 oz) cocoa
2 teaspoons baking soda
175 g (6 oz) light brown sugar
1 egg, beaten
75 ml (3 fl oz) vegetable oil
150 ml (¼ pint) buttermilk
75 ml (3 fl oz) boiling water
125 g (4 oz) cream cheese
100 g (3½ oz) smooth peanut
  butter
200 g (7 oz) icing sugar
100 g (3½ oz) plain dark
  chocolate

- Line a large baking sheet with baking paper. Place the flour, cocoa, baking soda and light brown sugar in a large bowl. Mix the egg, oil and buttermilk with the boiling water and stir into the dry ingredients until well mixed. Spoon about 30 tablespoonfuls on to the tray, making sure they are well spaced, and bake in a preheated oven, 180°C (350°F), Gas Mark 4, for 10–12 minutes or until just firm. Leave to cool.

- Beat together the cream cheese and peanut butter until smooth. Sift in the icing sugar and beat until well combined. Pipe or spoon over the icing over 15 halves, then sandwich the remaining 15 on top.

- Melt the chocolate over a small bowl set in a pan of simmering water, making sure the water does not touch the bottom of the bowl. Drizzle over the whoopie pies before serving.

---

1 Chocolate Peanut Butter Shakes

For each shake, whizz 2 scoops of vanilla ice cream with 200 ml (7 fl oz) milk, 3 tablespoons peanut butter and 4 tablespoons ready-made chocolate sauce until smooth. Pour into a large glass and top with some whipped cream and a roughly chopped peanut chocolate bar.

2 Chocolate Peanut Butter Bites

Stamp out 12 rounds from a 375 g (12 oz) sheet of ready-rolled shortcrust pastry and use them to line a lightly greased 12-hole mini-muffin tray. Bake in a preheated oven, 200°C (400°F), Gas Mark 6, for 10 minutes or until golden. Press any puffed sides down with a teaspoon.

Meanwhile, heat 25 g (1 oz) butter, 50 ml (2 fl oz) double cream, 100 g (3½ oz) white chocolate and 50 g (2 oz) peanut butter in a pan over a very low heat until smooth. Pour a little into each tart case and place in the freezer to cool. Melt 50 g (2 oz) plain dark chocolate in a bowl over a pan of simmering water and drizzle over to serve.

30 Individual Pear Crumbles with Flapjack Topping

Serves 4

75 ml (3 fl oz) good-quality apple sauce
4 Conference pears, peeled, cored and chopped
½ teaspoon ground cinnamon
50 g (2 oz) soft brown sugar
75 g (3 oz) plain flour
50 g (2 oz) rolled oats
75 g (3 oz) butter
1 tablespoon golden syrup

- Put the apple sauce, pears and cinnamon into a small saucepan and gently cook for 10 minutes until softened. Spoon the mixture into 4 ramekins or ovenproof teacups.

- Rub together the sugar, flour, oats and butter to make a lumpy mixture. Stir in the golden syrup. Scatter on top of the fruit and bake in a preheated oven, 200°C (400°F), Gas Mark 6, for 15 minutes until golden and bubbling.

1 Pear and Flapjack Parfait

Finely chop 2 pears and simmer in 50 ml (2 fl oz) water with 1 tablespoon lemon juice, a pinch of cinnamon and 25 g (1 oz) soft brown sugar for 5 minutes. Tip into a metal bowl and cool in the freezer. Mix together 300 ml (½ pint) Greek yogurt with 1 teaspoon vanilla extract and 2 tablespoons caster sugar. Place a spoonful of the pear at the bottom of 4 serving dishes. Spoon over some yogurt, then top with some crumbled flapjack. Repeat the layers, ending with a sprinkling of flapjack and some toasted flaked almonds.

2 Baked Pear with Crumble Topping

Heat 25 g (1 oz) butter in a large frying pan. Add 4 peeled, halved and cored pears and cook for 5 minutes, then pour over 4 tablespoons orange juice and cook for 2 minutes more. Meanwhile, heat 50 g (2 oz) butter and 2 tablespoons honey in a saucepan, then stir in 50 g (2 oz) oats. Put the pears on a baking sheet, cut side up, and scatter over the oat mixture. Bake in a preheated oven, 200°C (400°F), Gas Mark 6, for 5–10 minutes until the topping is crunchy and the pears are soft. Serve with vanilla ice cream.

Banana Pecan Strudels

Serves 4

4 sheets of filo pastry

50 g (2 oz) butter, melted

4 tablespoons icing sugar

25 g (1 oz) pecans, toasted and
finely chopped

2 bananas, sliced lengthways
into quarters

100 g (3½ oz) mascarpone
cheese

2 tablespoons maple syrup,
plus extra for drizzling

- Unroll a pastry sheet, keeping the remainder covered with a damp but not wet cloth. Brush all over with some butter, then sift over 1 tablespoon of the icing sugar and scatter with one-quarter of the pecans. Cut in half and place a banana quarter along both shorter ends. Fold in the long edges and roll up. Place on a baking sheet and repeat with the remaining pastry.

- Brush all over with more butter, then cook in a preheated oven, 200°C (400°F), Gas Mark 6, for 12–15 minutes until crisp and golden.

- Mix the mascarpone with the maple syrup and serve alongside the pastries with more maple syrup drizzled over.

 Warm Fudge and Banana Pecan

Splits Put 50 g (2 oz) butter, 100 g (3½ oz) soft brown sugar and 125 ml (4 fl oz) double cream in a pan, bring to the boil and simmer for 5 minutes. Cut 4 bananas in half and place in serving dishes. Top with scoops of vanilla ice cream, then drizzle over the sauce. Sprinkle over 25 g (1 oz) toasted pecans before serving.

 Banana Pecan Crumble

Slice 4 bananas and mix with 75 ml (3 fl oz) each ready-made caramel sauce and double cream. Place in an ovenproof dish. Whizz together 125 g (4 oz) each plain flour, light brown sugar and butter in a food processor until the mixture resembles breadcrumbs. Stir in 50 g (2 oz) rolled oats and 25 g (1 oz) desiccated coconut. Scatter over the bananas and cook in a preheated oven, 180°C (350°F), Gas Mark 4, for 25 minutes or until golden and bubbling.

30 Lemon Puddings

Serves 4

50 g (2 oz) butter
125 g (4 oz) caster sugar
2 eggs, separated
50 g (2 oz) plain flour
150 ml (¼ pint) milk
150 ml (¼ pint) single cream
finely grated rind of 1 lemon and juice of ½ lemon
icing sugar, to serve

- Put the butter and sugar in a bowl and beat with a hand-held electric whisk until pale and creamy. Add the egg yolks and mix in well, then stir in the flour. Gradually whisk in the milk and cream, followed by the lemon rind and juice.

- Whisk the egg whites until stiff peaks form. Stir one-third of the whites into the batter. Then carefully fold in the remainder, half at a time. Spoon the mixture into 4 individual ramekins and bake in a preheated oven, 180°C (350°F), Gas Mark 4, for 15 minutes or until golden. Dust with icing sugar to serve.

1 Lemon Baskets
Mix together 200 g (7 oz) crème fraîche and 125 g (4 oz) lemon curd until smooth. Spoon into 4 ready-made brandy snap baskets. Scatter a handful of blackberries on top, dust with icing sugar and serve.

2 Lemon Mousse
Using a hand-held electric whisk, mix together 300 ml (½ pint) double cream, 75 g (3 oz) caster sugar and the finely grated rind of 1 lemon. Stir in 1 tablespoon lemon juice or to taste and whisk until smooth.

Whisk 2 egg whites until stiff peaks form. Stir a spoonful of the mixture into the whipped cream, then carefully fold in the remainder, half at a time. Spoon into serving bowls and grate over some more lemon rind to serve.

Seared Pineapple with Rum and Coconut

Serves 6

25 g (1 oz) butter
50 g (2 oz) soft brown sugar
1 pineapple, peeled and cut into wedges
2 tablespoons rum
25 g (1 oz) desiccated or curled coconut
coconut or vanilla ice cream, to serve

- Heat the butter in a large frying pan until melted. Sprinkle half the sugar over the pineapple and cook for 3 minutes until caramelized. Turn the wedges over and cook for 2 minutes more. Remove the pineapple from the pan.

- Take the frying pan off the heat and add the rum and remaining sugar. Return to the heat and simmer until thickened.

- Meanwhile, place the coconut in a small, dry frying pan and cook for 1–2 minutes, stirring frequently, until lightly browned. Put the pineapple slices on serving plates with scoops of ice cream. Drizzle over the sauce and scatter over the coconut to serve.

 Pineapple Pancakes with Coconut Sauce Mix 200 g (7 oz) self-raising flour with 1 teaspoon baking powder and a pinch of salt. Beat in 1 egg and 300 ml (½ pint) milk. Heat a little butter in a nonstick frying pan. Add 3 tablespoonfuls of batter. Place a pineapple ring on top of each and cook for 2–3 minutes on each side until puffed and golden. Keep warm and repeat with the remaining mixture. Meanwhile, mix 50 g (2 oz) caster sugar with a little water, heat for 2 minutes until melted and cook until dark gold. Remove from heat and stir in 150 ml (5 fl oz) coconut milk. Heat through and spoon over the pancakes.

 Individual Pineapple and Coconut Cakes Grease 6 large ramekins and coat with 1 tablespoon caster sugar, shaking away any excess. Place 1 canned pineapple ring in the bottom of each ramekin. In a food processor, whizz together 150 g (5 oz) each of softened butter, caster sugar and self-raising flour with 2 eggs and 50 g (2 oz) coconut cream until smooth. Spoon the batter into the ramekins and bake in a preheated oven, 180°C (350°F), Gas Mark 4, for 20–25 minutes until just cooked through. Meanwhile, melt 50 g (2 oz) each of butter and soft brown sugar in a pan. Cook for 2–3 minutes then take off the heat and carefully pour in 2 tablespoons rum. Turn out the cakes on to plates and spoon over the sauce.

 # Raspberry Tiramisu

Serves 4

2 egg yolks
50 g (2 oz) caster sugar
4 tablespoons Marsala
300 ml (½ pint) double cream
250 g (8 oz) mascarpone cheese
125 ml (4 fl oz) strong coffee,
  cooled
16 sponge fingers
50 g (2 oz) plain dark chocolate,
  grated
200 g (7 oz) raspberries

- Put the egg yolks and 2 tablespoons each sugar and Marsala into a small bowl set over a pan of simmering water, making sure the bottom of the bowl does not touch the water. Whisk the mixture until fluffy and it holds a trail when the whisk is lifted out of the bowl. Keep whisking until cooled.

- Whisk the cream until soft peaks form. Beat together the mascarpone and the remaining sugar and stir this into the cooled egg mixture, followed by the whipped cream.

- Put the coffee and remaining Marsala into a shallow bowl. Dip some of the sponge fingers in the mixture and place in the bottom of 4 serving bowls. Scatter over some chocolate and raspberries, then spoon over some of the cream mixture. Repeat the layers until the mixture is used up. Top with grated chocolate to serve.

 Crunchy Raspberry Mess

Lightly crush 3 individual meringue nests. Mix together 200 g (7 oz) mascarpone cheese with 150 ml (¼ pint) fresh custard. Stir together with the crushed meringue and 150 g (5 oz) raspberries. Place in serving bowls and grate over some plain dark chocolate before serving.

 Raspberry Mascarpone Puffs

Cut out 4 rounds, each 5 cm (2 inches) across, from a sheet of ready-rolled puff pastry. Place on a lightly greased baking sheet and brush all over with egg yolk. Cook in a preheated oven, 200°C (400°F), Gas Mark 6, for 10–15 minutes until golden and crisp. Leave to cool. Mix together 250 g (8 oz)

mascarpone cheese, 2–3 tablespoons caster sugar and 1 teaspoon vanilla extract. Spoon the mixture over the cooled pastry. Scatter with a handful of raspberries and some chocolate curls to serve.

30 White Chocolate Rice Pudding Brûlée

Serves 4

125 g (4 oz) pudding rice
250 ml (8 fl oz) milk
300 ml (½ pint) single cream
50 g (2 oz) plus 4 tablespoons
  caster sugar
1 teaspoon vanilla extract
2 egg yolks
75 g (3 oz) white chocolate,
  chopped

- Cook the rice in a large saucepan of boiling water for 5 minutes and drain well. Return to the pan and pour over the milk, cream, 50 g (2 oz) sugar and the vanilla extract. Cook over a medium heat for 15–20 minutes until soft and creamy. Remove from the heat and stir through the egg yolks and white chocolate until smooth.

- Spoon the mixture into 4 individual heatproof ramekins and smooth over the top with the spoon. Leave to cool a little, then scatter over the remaining caster sugar. Place under a preheated hot grill and cook for 1 minute until the sugar caramelizes. Leave to cool until the surface is hard, then serve.

 White Chocolate Crispy Rice Squares

Melt 50 g (2 oz) butter and 100 g (3½ oz) white chocolate in a saucepan. Add 300 g (10 oz) marshmallows and stir until melted, then add 200 g (7 oz) puffed rice cereal and stir until well coated. Line a 20 × 30 cm (8 × 12 inch) baking tin with baking paper and pour in the mixture. Leave to cool, then cut into squares and pile on to plates to serve.

 Chocolate Custard and Rice Tarts

Melt 75 g (3 oz) white chocolate in a bowl over a pan of gently simmering water and leave to cool a little. Mix 200 ml (7 fl oz) ready-cooked rice pudding and 300 ml (½ pint) fresh custard with 1 egg yolk. Stir in the chocolate and 25 g (1 oz) raisins. Spoon into 4 ready-made tart cases and bake in a preheated oven, 180°C (350°F), Gas Mark 4, for 12–15 minutes until the mixture is just set. Dust with a little ground cinnamon to serve.

1 Apple, Maple and Pecan Fool

Serves 4

200 g (7 oz) good-quality apple
sauce
1 Granny Smith apple, peeled and
grated or finely chopped
200 ml (7 fl oz) double cream
250 ml (8 fl oz) fresh custard
3 tablespoons maple syrup
25 g (1 oz) pecans, toasted and
chopped
pecan biscuits, to serve

- Put the apple sauce and apple in a small saucepan, cook for 5 minutes to soften, then place in metal bowl in the freezer for a few minutes to cool.

- Whip the cream until soft peaks form, then stir in the custard. Swirl through the apple purée and maple syrup, then spoon into serving dishes. Top with toasted pecans and serve with pecan biscuits.

2 Apple and Pecan Brioches

Core and thinly slice 2 Braeburn apples, arrange on a baking sheet and brush over a little melted butter. Cook under a preheated medium grill for 3 minutes on each side until lightly golden. Mix 150 ml (5 fl oz) each of milk and cream with 1 egg and 1 teaspoon vanilla extract. Dip 8 slices of brioche in the mixture until well coated. Heat a little butter in a nonstick frying pan and cook the brioche in batches for 2–3 minutes on each side until golden. Arrange the apple slices on top, add spoonfuls of crème fraîche and scatter over chopped pecans. Drizzle with a little maple syrup to serve.

3 Apple and Pecan Tart

Unwrap a 375 g (12 oz) sheet of ready-rolled puff pastry on to a lightly greased baking sheet. Score around the edge with a sharp knife, taking care not to cut right through the pastry, to make a 1 cm (½ inch) border. Brush over this border with 1 beaten egg. Core and slice 6 Granny Smith apples. Toss with 1 teaspoon ground cinnamon and 2 tablespoons caster sugar and scatter over the tart. Cook in a preheated oven, 200°C (400°F), Gas Mark 6, for 20 minutes, then scatter over 25 g (1 oz) chopped pecans and cook for 2 minutes more until crisp and lightly golden. Drizzle over 2 tablespoons maple syrup and serve.

30 Strawberry Rhubarb Shortcake Slices

Serves 4–6

100 g (3½ oz) cold butter, cubed, plus extra for greasing
300 g (10 oz) plain flour
1 tablespoon baking powder
3 tablespoons caster sugar
1 egg, beaten
150 ml (¼ pint) milk
100 g (3½ oz) rhubarb, trimmed and sliced
50 g (2 oz) soft brown sugar
finely grated rind of 1 orange
100 ml (3½ fl oz) port
300 ml (½ pint) double cream
150 g (5 oz) strawberries

- Lightly grease a baking sheet. Put the butter, flour, baking powder and 2 tablespoons caster sugar in a large bowl or food processor. Rub or blend together until the mixture resembles coarse breadcrumbs. Mix together the egg and milk and pour into the bowl. Cut through the mixture with a fork until it is just combined. Roll out the dough on a lightly floured surface until it is about 10 × 20 cm (4 × 8 inches), trimming the edges. Place on the baking sheet and bake in a preheated oven, 180°C (350°F), Gas Mark 4, for 15–20 minutes until golden. Leave to cool.

- Meanwhile, put the rhubarb, soft brown sugar, orange rind and port in a saucepan with a splash of water, cover and cook for 5 minutes, then cook for 5 minutes more uncovered until the rhubarb is soft. Place in a metal bowl in the freezer and leave to cool.

- Whip the cream and the remaining caster sugar until soft peaks form. Place the shortcake on a serving dish. Swirl over the whipped cream, spoon over the compote and arrange the strawberries on top. Cut into slices to serve.

 1 **Rhubarb Strawberry Dunkers** Whizz together 150 g (5 oz) hulled strawberries in a food processor with 50 g (2 oz) canned rhubarb and sugar to taste until a smooth sauce forms. Stir through 200 g (7 oz) ricotta and divide between 6 serving bowls. Drizzle over 1 tablespoon honey and serve with shortbread biscuits for dunking.

 2 **Strawberry and Rhubarb Tarts** Cut a 375 g (12 oz) sheet of ready-rolled puff pastry into 6 rectangles. Mix together 50 g (2 oz) crème fraîche with 4 tablespoons caster sugar and spread over the centre of each rectangle. Top with 75 g (3 oz) sliced rhubarb and 125 g (4 oz) halved strawberries. Sift over 3 tablespoons icing sugar and bake in a preheated oven, 220°C (425°F), Gas Mark 7, for 15 minutes until golden.

30 Caramelized Custard Tarts

Serves 4

375 g (12 oz) sheet ready-rolled
 puff pastry
pinch of ground nutmeg
½ teaspoon ground cinnamon
2 tablespoons caster sugar

Filling

3 egg yolks
50 g (2 oz) caster sugar
2 tablespoons cornflour
1 teaspoon vanilla extract
finely grated rind of ¼ lemon
300 ml (½ pint) double cream

- Unwrap the pastry and sprinkle over the nutmeg, cinnamon and 2 tablespoons caster sugar. Then tightly roll up the pastry, like a Swiss roll, and cut it into 12 x 1.5 cm (¾ inch) slices (you may have some pastry left over). Roll each slice into a small round on a lightly floured surface. Turn a 12-hole muffin tin upside down, gently press each round over the top of a muffin mould and chill in the freezer for 5 minutes.

- Bake in a preheated oven, 220°C (425°F), Gas Mark 7, for 5 minutes, then place the pastry cases on a baking tray.

- Meanwhile, for the filling, put the egg yolks, the caster sugar, cornflour, vanilla extract and lemon rind in a bowl and whisk until smooth. Add the cream and whisk again, then cook in a saucepan for 5 minutes, stirring frequently, until the mixture is thick, taking care not to let it boil. Spoon the custard into the pastry cases. Turn up the oven to 230°C (450°F), Gas Mark 8, and bake for 12–15 minutes until caramelized and set.

---

1 Creamy Caramel
Whip 300 ml (½ pint) double cream until soft peaks form, then stir in 3 tablespoons ready-made caramel sauce. Spoon into 4 serving bowls. Sprinkle over a little ground cinnamon and drizzle with some more caramel sauce. Serve with tuile biscuits.

2 Caramel and Banana Tart
In a food processor, whizz 300 g (10 oz) oaty biscuits until small crumbs form, then pulse in 75 g (3 oz) melted butter. Press into a 23 cm (9 inch) tart tin and cook in a preheated oven, 180°C (350°F), Gas Mark 4, for 10–12 minutes until golden and crisp.

Leave to cool a little, then spread 6 tablespoons dulce de leche on top. Slice 2 bananas and place on top of the sauce. Whip 300 ml (½ pint) double cream with 1 tablespoon caster sugar. Spoon over the bananas and top with a little grated chocolate.

 # Warm Chocolate Cherry Tarts

Serves 4

200 g (7 oz) plain dark chocolate, broken into pieces
3 tablespoons double cream
1 tablespoon brandy
2 eggs and 1 egg yolk
50 g (2 oz) caster sugar
50 g (2 oz) undyed glacé cherries, halved
4 ready-made individual pastry cases

- Put the chocolate, cream and brandy in a small bowl. Set it over a saucepan of gently simmering water, so the bottom of the bowl is not touching the water, and heat for a couple of minutes until the chocolate is melted. Leave to cool a little.

- Whisk together the eggs, egg yolk and sugar with a hand-held electric whisk until pale and creamy. Carefully stir the chocolate mixture into the eggs. Arrange the cherries in the pastry cases, pour over the chocolate mixture and bake in a preheated oven, 190°C (375°F), Gas Mark 5, for 12 minutes or until just set.

 Cherries with Chocolate Dipping Sauce Heat 200 ml (7 fl oz) double cream in a pan until boiling. Put 200 g (7 oz) chopped plain dark chocolate in a bowl. Pour the cream over and stir until smooth. Add a splash of brandy or kirsch, if liked. Place in a warm serving bowl and serve with fresh cherries for dunking.

 Individual Chocolate Cherry Cakes Put 150 g (5 oz) each softened butter and caster sugar, 125 g (4 oz) self-raising flour, 25 g (1 oz) cocoa powder, 3 eggs, 3 tablespoons milk and 1 teaspoon baking powder in a food processor and whizz until smooth. Butter and flour 4 ramekins and spoon the mixture into them. Bake in a preheated oven, 180°C (350°F), Gas Mark 4, for 12–15 minutes until just cooked through. Turn the cakes out and leave to cool. Meanwhile, whip 200 ml (7 fl oz) double cream with 2 tablespoons icing sugar. Stone 150 g (5 oz) fresh cherries. Cut each cake in half horizontally. Spread a little cream over the bottom halves and add 1 teaspoon cherry jam to each. Top with the other halves, then spoon more cream on top and finish with some fresh cherries.

3⊖ Passionfruit Cheesecakes

Serves 6

150 g (5 oz) gingernut biscuits, crushed
50 g (2 oz) butter, melted, plus extra for greasing
400 g (13 oz) cream cheese
75 g (3 oz) icing sugar, sifted
2 teaspoons vanilla extract
200 ml (7 fl oz) double cream
3 passionfruit

- Mix together the crushed gingernuts and butter. Place 6 metal rings, each 9 cm (3½ inches) across, on serving plates. Alternatively, cut 12 strips of baking paper and place 2 in a cross-shape in the bottom of 6 lightly greased individual ramekins, leaving the ends hanging over the sides. Press the crumbs into the bottom of the rings or ramekins and put them in the freezer while you make the filling.

- Beat together the cream cheese, icing sugar and vanilla extract until smooth. Then beat in the double cream until the mixture thickens. Spoon the mixture into the rings or ramekins and return to the freezer until firmly set, about 10 minutes.

- Carefully ease the rings off the cheesecakes or lift them from the ramekins using the baking paper. Scoop out the passionfruit pulp and spoon over the cheesecakes to serve.

1⊖ Bananas in Passionfruit and Ginger Syrup

Put 150 ml (5 fl oz) passionfruit pulp in a small saucepan with a knob of peeled fresh root ginger, 100 ml (3½ fl oz) each sweet dessert wine and water and 75 g (3 oz) caster sugar and boil for 5 minutes until syrupy. Remove the ginger. Halve 6 bananas and place them in serving bowls. Spoon over the warm syrup and serve with yogurt.

2⊖ Passionfruit Curd Pots

Place 150 ml (5 fl oz) passionfruit pulp in a pan along with 175 g (6 oz) butter, 200 g (7 oz) caster sugar and 1 tablespoon lemon juice and warm to melt the butter. Whisk together 3 eggs and 2 egg yolks. Add 2 tablespoons of the passionfruit pulp and stir together, then pour all the mixture back into the pan. Cook over a low heat for 3–5 minutes or until the mixture has thickened. Pour into a bowl and chill in the refrigerator. Lightly crush 125 g (4 oz) gingernut biscuits and put them in the bottom of 6 serving glasses. Whisk 250 ml (8 fl oz) double cream until soft peaks form and stir together with 2 tablespoons icing sugar and 200 ml (7 fl oz) mascarpone cheese. Layer the cream mixture in the glasses with the passionfruit curd, topping with some fresh passionfruit pulp.

 # Warm Mango and Raspberry Gratin

Serves 4

125 ml (4 fl oz) double cream
150 g (5 oz) mascarpone cheese
200 g (7 oz) ready-made pastry
  cream
1 mango, peeled, pitted and sliced
250 g (8 oz) raspberries

- Whip the cream until soft peaks form, then carefully stir together with the mascarpone and pastry cream.

- Put the mango and raspberries in a small, shallow ovenproof dish and spread the cream mixture on top. Cook very close to a hot grill for 2–3 minutes until lightly browned.

 Mango and Raspberry Pastry Stacks Cut 325 g (11 oz) ready-rolled puff pastry into 12 rectangles and place on a baking sheet. Cover with another baking sheet and cook in a preheated oven, 200°C (400°F), Gas Mark 6, for 10 minutes or until golden and crisp. Uncover and sift over 2 tablespoons icing sugar. Place under a hot grill for 30 seconds until the sugar melts, then leave to cool. Mix together 150 ml (5 fl oz) double cream, whipped to soft peaks, with 200 g (7 oz) mascarpone cheese, 3 tablespoons icing sugar and 1 teaspoon vanilla extract. Place 4 pastry pieces on serving plates. Spoon over some cream and arrange mango slices and raspberries on top. Repeat the layers, finishing with a piece of pastry.

 Mango Cakes with Raspberry Sauce Butter 4 individual ramekins or dariole moulds. Mix together 2 tablespoons each softened butter and soft brown sugar and spoon the mixture into the bottom of the ramekins. Add 1 tablespoon chopped mango to each ramekin. Whizz together 100 g (3½ oz) each softened butter, caster sugar and self-raising flour with 2 eggs and 1 teaspoon vanilla extract until a smooth batter forms. Spoon the batter into the ramekins and cook in a preheated oven, 180°C (350°F), Gas Mark 4, for 20–25 minutes until just cooked through. Press 150 g (5 oz) raspberries through a sieve and sift in 1 tablespoon icing sugar to make a sauce. Spoon the sauce over the cakes to serve.

30 Sticky Orange and Cinnamon Puddings

Serves 4

100 g (3½ oz) butter, softened, plus extra for greasing

4 tablespoon golden syrup, plus extra for serving

2 large oranges

100 g (3½ oz) soft brown sugar

150 g (5 oz) self-raising flour

½ teaspoon ground cinnamon

2 eggs

- Grease 4 individual pudding moulds or ramekins and divide the golden syrup between them. Finely grate the rind of both oranges and place in a food processor, then use a sharp knife to remove the pith. Thickly slice 1 orange. Carefully arrange 1 orange slice at the bottom of each mould. Chop the remaining orange flesh, removing any pith or seeds, and place in the food processor together with the remaining ingredients. Whizz to make a smooth batter.

- Spoon the batter into the moulds. Place in a roasting tin half-filled with boiling water. Cover with kitchen foil and bake in a preheated oven, 180°C (350°F), Gas Mark 4, for 20–25 minutes until just cooked through. Leave for a minute in the moulds, then turn out on to plates and serve with a little more golden syrup drizzled over if liked.

10 Caramel Oranges with Cinnamon Yogurt

Heat 75 g (3 oz) soft brown sugar in a large frying pan with 75 ml (3 fl oz) double cream and 25 g (1 oz) butter until the butter has melted. Peel and thickly slice 6 oranges and add to the pan. Swirl the sauce over the oranges and cook for a further 2 minutes. Spoon out on to plates. Mix 150 g (5 oz) natural yogurt together with 1 teaspoon cinnamon and spoon over the oranges before serving.

20 Orange and Cinnamon Tart

Unwrap a 375 g (12 oz) pack of ready-rolled shortcrust or dessert pastry on to a lightly greased baking sheet, crimp around the edges and bake in a preheated oven, 200°C (400°F), Gas Mark 6, for 12 minutes or until golden and crisp. Leave to cool. Stir 200 g (7 oz) cream cheese with the finely grated rind and juice of 1 orange, 1 teaspoon cinnamon and 2 tablespoons icing sugar. Spoon over the pastry. Peel and slice 2 oranges and arrange the slices on top.

 Honey Ricotta Fritters with Pistachios

Serves 4

200 g (7 oz) ricotta
1 egg, lightly beaten
50 g (2 oz) plain flour
25 g (1 oz) caster sugar
finely grated rind and juice of
  1 orange
oil, for frying
5 tablespoons clear honey
25 g (1 oz) pistachios, chopped
salt
Greek yogurt, to serve (optional)

- Drain any water from the ricotta, then mix it with the egg until smooth. Stir in the flour, sugar and orange rind together with a pinch of salt.

- Fill a large saucepan one-third full of oil and heat it until a small piece of bread dropped in the oil sizzles and turns brown after 15 seconds. Drop spoonfuls of the ricotta mixture into the oil and cook for 1–2 minutes until golden and puffed. Leave to drain on kitchen paper.

- Meanwhile, heat the orange juice and honey in a small saucepan until well combined. Place the warm fritters on serving plates and drizzle over the honey syrup. Scatter over the chopped pistachios and serve with yogurt, if liked.

 Fresh Fruit with Honey Ricotta Dip

Stir together 200 g (7 oz) ricotta, 1 tablespoon clear honey and 1 teaspoon vanilla extract. Place in a serving bowl, scatter over some chopped pistachios and serve with strawberries and melon slices for dipping.

 Ricotta Puddings with Honey Syrup

Whisk 2 egg whites until stiff peaks form. Drain any water from 250 g (8 oz) ricotta and beat together with 2 tablespoons caster sugar and 1 teaspoon vanilla extract until smooth. Stir in a large spoonful of the egg white, then carefully fold in the remaining egg white, half at a time. Lightly grease 4 individual ramekins. Spoon the ricotta mixture into them and bake in a preheated oven, 160°C (325°F), Gas Mark 3, for 20 minutes or until a skewer inserted into the centre of a pudding comes out clean. Leave for a minute, then turn out on to plates. Drizzle over 4 tablespoons clear honey and scatter with some chopped pistachios.

Index

Italic pagination indicates photographs

Acknowledgements

Recipes by **Emma Lewis**
Executive Editor **Eleanor Maxfield**
Project Editor **Alex Stetter**
Art Direction **Tracy Killick for Tracy Killick Art Direction and Design**
Original design concept **www.gradedesign.com**
Designer **Sally Bond for Tracy Killick Art Direction and Design**
Photographer **Will Heap**
Home Economist **Emma Lewis**
Prop Stylist **Liz Hippisley**
Production Controller **Sarah Kramer**